D1085092

SIGN DESIGN
GALLERY

ROCKPORT
PUBLISHERS

Rockport Publishers · Rockport, Massachusetts

First published in the United States of America by:
Rockport Publishers, Inc.
146 Granite Street
Rockport, Massachusetts 01966
Telephone: (508) 546-9590
Fax: (508) 546-7141
Telex: 5106019284 ROCKORT PUB

Distributed to the book trade and art trade in the U.S. and Canada by:
North Light, an imprint of
F & W Publications
1507 Dana Avenue
Cincinnati, Ohio 45207
Telephone: (513) 531-2222

Other Distribution by:
Rockport Publishers, Inc.
Rockport, Massachusetts 01966

ISBN 1-56496-070-6

10 9 8 7 6 5 4 3 2 1

Designer: Carolyn Letvin/Letvin Design
Editor: Rosalie Grattaroti
Production Manager: Barbara States
Production Assistant: Pat O'Maley
ST Production Editor: Mark Kissling/ST Publications

Special thanks to Tod Swormstedt,
Group Publisher at Sign of the Times
Publications, Cincinnato, Ohio.

Printed in Hong Kong

CONTENTS

INTRODUCTION 4

GROUND SIGNS 5

PROJECTING OR HANGING SIGNS 33

POST- OR POLE-MOUNTED SIGNS 57

ENTRY MONUMENTS 77

SIGN SYSTEMS 89

WALL-MOUNT OR FACIA SIGNS 101

SPECIALTY SIGNS 131

INDEX 158

INTRODUCTION

SIGNS OF THE TIMES, the sign industry's leading journal since 1906, has followed the trends in sign design for more than 80 years. In SIGN DESIGN GALLERY, the editors of SIGNS OF THE TIMES have drawn from the banks of their annual design contests in order to capsulize the state-of-the-art for this last decade of the century.

The collection of photos that follows runs the gamut of current design trends. The reader will see the period looks of art deco, art nouveau and Victorian eras with their emphasis on fine detail and embellishment as well as the clean and polished look of "less is more" modern design. Every sort of material known to the sign designer's palette is in evidence, complimented by the myriad techniques available to the craftspeople who fabricate. Rough sawn cedar appears alongside stainless steel; hand-formed neon stands next to carved and gilded glass.

By bringing the techniques and materials together in their real and working environments, SIGNS OF THE TIMES has created a veritable idea book of successful solutions for not only the sign industry, but the design community at-large and their clients as well.

GROUND SIGNS

Ground signs are a broad category of signage defined by their free-standing nature: They are not attached to the buildings they identify. For the purposes of this book, ground signs include both low-profile and pylon signs, two types of signage which are characterized by their invisible means of support. The more specialized categories of free-standing signs—entry monuments, post- and pole-mounted signs, and sign systems—are reviewed in their own respective chapters.

Designer
Andre Probst Creative Design Inc.
Kitchener, ON, Canada

Fabricator
Andre Probst Creative Design Inc.

This 5-ft. diameter globe was fabricated of aluminum sheet, hand-formed to the correct radius and geographically accurate within one inch. The globe was welded to a tubular aluminum frame representing given longitudinal and latitudinal rings, and tilted at the correct angle. It was finished in a copper metallic acrylic enamel, complementing the 8-ft. high sheetmetal base, which has been "marbled" by acid treatment and finished in a transparent color coat.

Designer
Douglas Williams
Douglas Williams Woodcarving
Honolulu, HI

Fabricator
Douglas Williams Woodcarving

This entire 3 x 10-ft. double-sided sign was fabricated from high-density foam. Portions are stucco-textured. The raised letters were brushed with stainless steel.

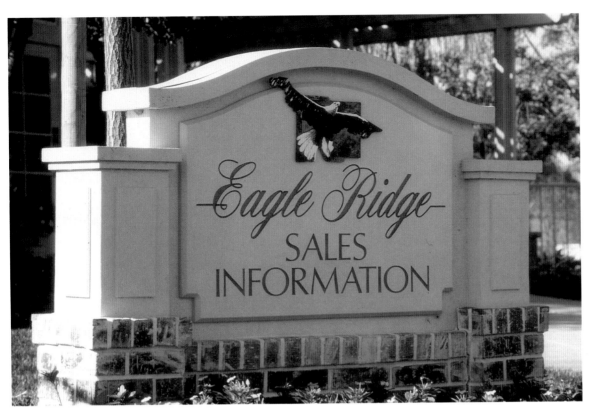

Designer
Jon Wanbaugh
Outdoor Dimensions
Anaheim, CA

Fabricator
Outdoor Dimensions

This sign was sandblasted and filled with goldleaf. A hand-painted applique made of high-density foam works to enhance the overall appeal of this avante garde signage program.

Designer
Gary Anderson
Bloomington Design
Bloomington, IN

Fabricator
Bloomington Design

Layers of MDO plywood were painted with enamel and applied to a cedar base on this 4 x 4-ft. sign.

Designer
Sign Crafters, Inc.
Lancaster, SC

Fabricator
Sign Crafters, Inc.

This sign is an internally-illuminated, double-face cabinet, fabricated from aluminum, with 1/2-in. clear push-through acrylic letters and logo. The color highlights on the logo and letters were achieved by using translucent vinyl. Measurements: 6 x 6 1/2 ft. with radius ends; 1 1/2 and 3-in. reveals.

Designer
Scott Bouma
Scott's Signs
Grandville, MI

Fabricators
Scott's Signs
Gary Carlson (carved fish)
Grandville, MI

This 36 x 60-in. solid-wood sign features a clear-coated background, airbrushing and enamel lettering. The hand-carved, hand-painted fish has a mechanical mouth and tail. It is 32 in. wide and 3 in. thick.

Designer
Mike Sheehan
Classic Sign & Mirror Inc.
Pensacola, FL

Fabricator
Classic Sign & Mirror Inc.

The pictoral and highlighted letters on this sign feature hand-blended colors. This 4 x 5-ft., double-sided, redwood sign was framed in stucco and mounted on a stucco base.

Designer
Andre Probst Creative Design Inc.
Kitchener, ON, Canada

Fabricators
Andre Probst Creative Design Inc.
Heritage Stoneworks
Kitchener, ON, Canada

This 66-in. ground sign was fabricated from concrete, glass block and 1/4-in.-thick aluminum letters; the logo was finished in acrylic enamel. Purple neon and floodlights were used for backlighting; frosted crystal film provides light diffusion for improved legibility of the graphics. The glass block has been laid with a gentle radius to maintain architectural integrity with the building's main entrance. Overall width: 112 in.

Designer
Mike Sheehan
Classic Sign & Mirror Inc.
Pensacola, FL

Fabricator
Classic Sign & Mirror Inc.

A wedge shape was used to make this 7-ft. double-faced sign. It features a lightweight, synthetic stucco structure. The redwood portion was lettered with carved, high-density foam, then finished in 23K goldleaf. Colors were chosen to complement the Florida sunset. The different elevations in the sign surfaces were outlined with a cove-routed 23K gold edge.

Designer
Tonia Marynell
Barntech Signs & Graphics
Sandersville, GA

Fabricator
Barntech Signs & Graphics

Mounted on 4 x 4-in. treated pine poles, this 3 x 9-ft. sandblasted redwood sign features a pictorial of the actual restaurant. From start to finish, the entire sign was completed in 33 hours.

Designer
Peter McGoldrick
Tigard, OR

Fabricator
Heath Signs
Portland, OR

Here, the goal was to complement the apartment complex's existing architecture. This internally illuminated sign (4 1/2 x 7 ft. cabinet; 8 ft. tall) was installed on a decorative, wood-trimmed base. The formed/embossed polycarbonate faces were reverse-painted.

Designer
Mark Taylor
Natural Graphics, Inc.
Houston, TX

Fabricator
Natural Graphics, Inc.

This stucco sign is just over 7 x 7 ft., and uses the same color scheme as the architecture of this Florida apartment community. The sign faces are sandblasted clear heart redwood with the birds hand-carved and applied. The logo as well as the sign was designed to create an upscale, yet casual image.

Designers
Mark Oatis
Smith, Nelson & Oatis
Denver, CO
Roybal Corp.
Denver, CO

Fabricators
Smith, Nelson & Oatis
Swanson Sheet Metal (metal work)
Denver, CO

Sheetmetal and PVC, in conjunction with an angle-iron frame, were used for this 6 x 3-ft. sign for an architectural firm. The finish was achieved with faux graphite in sign enamels, with faux incised copy.

Designer
John Stenko
Melweb
Daytona, FL

Fabricator
Federal Sign
Duluth, GA

This 10 x 16-ft. double-sided sign is of all aluminum construction. The name and stripe are internally illuminated.

Designer
Jon Wanbaugh
Outdoor Dimensions
Anaheim, CA

Fabricator
Outdoor Dimensions

This is a sandblasted wood sign with rod iron accents. The logo was hand-painted.

Designers
Karen Beane, Eric Federspiel
Rapid-Sign
Ft. Meyers, FL

Fabricator
Rapid-Sign

The cabinet for this 9 x 13-ft. monument sign was fabricated out of .090 aluminum with a polyurethane enamel finish. The aluminum faces were routed and painted. High-output fluorescent lamps illuminate the sign, and the continuous flow waterfall was illuminated with rods of aqua-marine neon.

Designer
Lawrin Rosen
ARTeffects, Inc.
Bloomfield, CT

Fabricator
ARTeffects, Inc.

The double-faced monolith features halo-lit letters and changeable panels of .125 aluminum. The illuminated cabinet is made of .063 aluminum with reverse sprayed polycarbonate faces. A light panel in the bottom of the cabinet allows light to spill over the lower messages.

Designer
Andrew Bollina
Cleveland Metroparks Graphics
Brecksville, OH

Fabricator
Cleveland Metroparks Graphics

This 60 x 66-in. all-basswood sign features a sandblasted background and a carved-and-routed banner. Rope was used for a nautical effect.

Designer
Paul McCarthy
Paul McCarthy's Carving Place
Scituate, MA

Fabricator
Paul McCarthy's Carving Place

This sign features 174 total individual carvings in low relief, keeping them lower than the lettering.

Designer
Peter Poanessa
Signwright
Walpole, NH

Fabricator
Signwright

This 30 in. x 8-ft., solid 2-in. mahogany sign serves a day care center. The globe and children were cut and laminated.

Designer
John Stenberg
Artsign Design
Boise, ID

Fabricator
Artsign Design

This 84 x 76-in. sandblasted, redwood sign for a new home subdivision features an airbrushed sky and foreground. The pictorial was hand-painted.

Designer
Peter A. Weingartner
Cincinnati, OH

Fabricator
Lackner Sign
Westchester, OH

This 6 x 8-ft. double-faced, internally illuminated sign features white flexible faces to which pressure-sensitive vinyl graphics are applied. The sign cabinet is constructed of an extruded aluminum and utilizes a click fastening system for the retainer faces which allows the faces to be replaced in the future.

Designer
Mike Sheehan
Classic Sign & Mirror
Pensacola, FL

Fabricator
Classic Sign & Mirror

Two 4-ft.-high tiger heads looking toward the road are the centerpieces of this 8 x 20-ft. double-sided sign. The plants, birds and tigers are carved from foam and finished with fiberglass. The graphics are one unit per side and mounted with a relief on a synthetic stucco structure carved to resemble rock.

Designers
Luttmann Brothers Woodcarving & Sign Co.
Phoenixville, PA
Firenze & Co.
Wilmington, DE

Fabricator
Luttmann Brothers Woodcarving & Sign Co.

The 69 x 79 1/2-in. sign board for this restaurant was executed in mahogany. The painted surface of the mahogany comprises four coats of two-part epoxy finished with four coats of two-part polyurethane (yacht finishes). Letters were carved and gilded with 23K gold. The seal was cast in polyurethane resins and coated with two-part epoxy and two-part polyurethane. The base of the seal is wood, and the ship was made of 14 individually cast pieces. Supporting poles are made of 2-in. steel.

Designer
Sign Consultants, Inc.
Minneapolis, MN

Fabricator
Cold Spring Granite
Cold Spring, MN

The logo sculpture of diamond pink granite is the focal point in this symmetrical building and landscape design. Polished and rough-finished surfaces create life and interest.

Designer
Noel Weber
Classic Sign Studio
Boise, ID

Fabricator
Classic Sign Studio

Fabricated from composite board for a historic site, this 5 x 3-ft. sign was marbled and sand-blasted.

Designer
Gary Stamper
Sign Service
Hayden Lake, ID

Fabricator
Sign Service

Mounted on a single pole, this double-faced sign comprises a sheetmetal cabinet with stucco finish. The neo-blue neon, double pan channel letters are backed by veep green neon. Overall size is 12 x 22 ft.

Designer
Jon Wanbaugh
Outdoor Dimensions
Anaheim, CA

Fabricator
Outdoor Dimensions

Fabricated with a brick base, a composite board box and face, this sign features a traditional design. The copy was sandblasted and painted; the logo is a cut-out, hand-painted applique.

Designer
Dana Hendel
Seattle, WA

Fabricator
Meyer Sign Co., Inc.
Seattle, WA

This 5 x 7-ft., low-profile monument display for a shopping center has a channel cabinet logo. The background of the tree cabinet was painted opaque and further enhanced with halo illumination. The logo cabinet was mounted to five fabricated aluminum strips, which gradate by both size and color. The copy, which was routed and projected with 1-in. black trim, is backlit by flourescent illumination.

Designer
Fritz Gompert
Progressive Image
Carmichael, CA

Fabricator
Progressive Image

Constructed of sheetmetal and finished in acrylic enamel with painted copy and graphics, this sign features a hand-painted pictorial. The body of the sign is elastomeric vinyl with cast plex numbers.

Designer
Monte G. Rogers
Edwardsburg, MI

Fabricator
Vince Rogers Signs
Elkhart, IN

This MDO sign for a restored historic home open to the public is approximately 4 x 6 ft. with the frame. The background effect was created by using flat black over gloss black. The lettering was gilded, with all but the underline of "Ruthmere" turned.

Designer
Luttmann Brothers Woodcarving & Sign Co.
Phoenixville, PA

Fabricator
Luttmann Brothers Woodcarving & Sign Co.

The entire sign for this townhouse group was fabricated from 18-lb. foam material. The trees were sculpted with a die grinder and various cutting bits. The sign panel is a box construction, with the 2 x 2-in. tubing that anchors the sign running up through the sign just shy of the top. The double-faced sign's dimensions: 7 x 37 1/2 x 57 in.

Designer
Larry Gipson
Federal Sign
Dublin, CA

Fabricator
Federal Sign

The cabinets and support elements are .090 aluminum, tex-coated and routed for graphics. Individual, illuminated channel letters were used in the pylon and tenant facia areas.

Designers
Glenn Silva
Glensign
Plymouth, MA
Hunt & Hulteen, Inc.
Brockton, MA

Fabricators
Glensign
Baysign
Plymouth, MA

This 5 x 7-ft., double-faced sign has a metal-ply face with a yellow vinyl background for nighttime visibility. Vinyl was also used to create the blue lines on the face, "enter" on the crayon, the ribbon, the copy and the vertical lines in the sign base. The crayon was made from a piece of 5-in. PVC pipe. The end of the crayon and the apple were made from high-density urethane. Copper was used on the leaf and the stem. The sign cap was fabricated from sugar pine. The sign base consists of 1 x 1-in. angle molding.

Designers
Woodmark
Akron, OH
Richard C. Foran (logo)
Akron, OH

Fabricator
Woodmark

This sign is 6 1/2 ft. tall x 4-ft. 9-in. wide x 5-in.-thick solid, laminated Douglas Fir with hand-carved graphics. It was finished with semi-transparent and opaque oil stains, enamel paint and goldleaf.

Designer
W.H. Goodwyn, III
Waverly, VA

Fabricator
Accent Signing Company
Virginia Beach, VA

Measuring 33 x 66 x 1 in., this sandblasted, clear heart redwood sign is encased in a wood frame of Georgian style with dental rail molding detail and a copper roof.

Designers
Robert Bogdan
Rustic Designs
Welland, ON, Canada
John Thompson (logo)
Welland, ON, Canada

Fabricator
Rustic Designs

Constructed of cedar, this 5 x 5-ft. sign features sandblasted lettering and a raised, cut-out and carved logo.

Designer
Yancey Sign Art, Inc.
Memphis, TN

Fabricator
Yancey Sign Art, Inc.

This 5 x 7-ft. double-faced, sandblasted, redwood sign is 12-in. thick. The leaves and tree were hand-carved.

Designer

Daniel Dillon
Dillon Design Associates
Cohoes, NY

Fabricator

Dillon Design Associates

A main entrance marker for a nursery and land-scaping service, this sign's overall size is 20 x 5 ft. It comprises sandblasted redwood with hand-carved 23K gilded lettering. The fading effect in the background was achieved by using three different colors.

Designers

Jay Cooke, Tracy Dunphy
Jay Cooke's Sign Shop
Stowe, VT

Fabricator

Jay Cooke's Sign Shop

This 5 x 7-ft. redwood sign has hand-carved letters outlined in 23K gold. The lily was sculpted and added on.

Designer
James B. Danieley, II
Greensboro, NC

Fabricator
Design Systems
Greensboro, NC

This sign is constructed from extruded aluminum and .125 thick aluminum panels. The posts are half round in design. The sign features reveals between signs and post which are painted red. The copy is precision cut from 1/2-in.-thick plate aluminum and mounted with concealed threaded rods.

Designer
Full Moon Signs & Graphics
Tallahassee, FL

Fabricator
Full Moon Signs & Graphics

Working from the client's existing logo, the designer created this 4 x 8-ft. sandblasted redwood sign. Mounted over MDO panels, the sign has an internal framework of press-treated pine. The recessed areas in the oval are hand-woven braided nylon ropes, simulating the screen mesh a T-shirt printer would use.

Designer
Merv Eckman
ADCON Signs
Ft. Collins, CO

Fabricator
ADCON Signs

There are two major parts to this double-faced dimensional sign. The center section features "The Square" name and stylized logo. The fan-shaped side sections identify the Center's major tenants. The sign is 24 ft. tall at street level and 20 ft. wide at the widest part of the fan sections.

Designer
Grate Signs, Inc.
Joliet, IL

Fabricator
Grate Signs, Inc.

Standing at the beginning of a 1/2-mile road that leads to a riverboat casino complex, this sign reaches a height of 45 ft. The identification portions of the sign are flexible vinyl faces decorated with pressure-sensitive vinyl graphics. The lower attraction board portion has track for 10 or 17-in. changeable copy.

Designers
John Stenberg, Randy Tolsma
Artsign Design
Boise, ID

Fabricator
Artsign Design

This 5 x 7-ft. sandblasted, redwood sign identifies a new home subdivision. The sky was airbrushed and the pictorial was hand-painted. The details in the eagle were stippled.

Designer
Julie Yashinski
Orde Advertising Co.
Green Bay, WI

Fabricator
Orde Advertising Co.

The overall height of this double-sided sign is 33 1/2 ft. The pylon is interior illuminated with white flexible face and applied vinyl copy. The building letters range from 2 1/2 ft. to 4 1/2 ft.

Designer
Joe Putjenter
Artistry Signs
Omaha, NE

Fabricator
Artistry Signs

Measuring 4 x 7 ft., this sign is comprised of composite board panels on each of the four sides and the top. The panels were glued and screwed into 4 x 4-in. cedar posts. The vinyl letters have painted outlines.

Designer
Peter Paanessa
Signwright
Walpole, NH

Fabricator
Signwright

The sign for this veterinary hospital, which measures 3 x 4 ft., was fabricated from mahogany. The oval was routed; the bear figure was cut-out and lami-nated.

Designers
Meredith Moquin, Lisa Hutchinson
Lawry Sign Inc.
Portsmouth, NH

Fabricators
Lawry Sign Inc.
Anchor Signs
Portsmouth, NH

This sign is 5 1/2 x 8-ft., double-sided, and internally-illuminated by fluorescent lights. It comprises four 8-in. steel poles, poly lattice work, and 23K gilded balls on top of the poles.

Designer
Signage, Inc.
Marysville, WA

Fabricator
Signage, Inc.

This is a custom brick constructed, three-wing monolith sign with detailing as per building architecture. The 12-in. letters are custom-milled, aluminum-plated and satin-textured. The center wing incorporates a 6 x 40-in. aluminum logo.

Designer
Steve Sinclaire
The Sicon Group/Adtronics
Richmond, BC, Canada

Fabricator
The Sicon Group/Adtronics

This double-faced display consists of a fabricated metal and aluminum structure, externally lit with ruby neon and floodlamps. The ID panel is a routed aluminum face, with the entire top of the radius being routed to achieve a halo effect. Overall dimensions are 14 1/2 x 19 ft.

PROJECTING OR HANGING SIGNS

Hanging and projecting signs represent one of the larger classifications of signage and are defined, as the terms suggest, by the method by which they are installed. Unlike ground signs, their placement and size are quite often dictated by the design of the buildings they identify. Hanging and projecting signs must be architecturally compatible, yet sufficiently visible to identify and promote the services or products within.

Designers
Rauh, Good, Darlo & Barnes
Los Gatos, CA
Gary Rhodes
Surfside Signs
Bellingham, WA

Fabricators
Surfside Signs
Forster Forge (steel bracket)
Santa Cruz, CA

The background of this sign was sandblasted; the sign face was chiseled and laminated. The mug, barley and center-panel copy was hand-carved from clear-heart redwood. The oval was hand-scoop-carved and gilded with 23K gold. The sign was painted to spec colors.

Designer
Michael Kinnunen
TubeArt
Seattle, WA

Fabricator
TubeArt

This single-faced, suspended sign (12 x 32-ft.) for retail shops in a convention center was fabricated from sheetmetal with multi-level backgrounds. The letters were fabricated to accommodate the multi-levels. The open pan-channel letters have exposed 4500 white neon within. The ribbon is formed aluminum with routed copy and pushed through 1/2-in. clear acrylic. The acrylic has polished edges and is backed by two tubes of 4500 white neon behind the ribbon.

Designer
Douglas Williams
Douglas Williams Woodcarving
Honolulu, HI

Fabricator
Douglas Williams Woodcarving

Two feet in diameter, the oak face and frame of this sign were painted white. The graphics were carved from high-density foam, painted and gilded with 23K gold with black edges.

Designer
Willie Wells
Signworld
Bridgewater, NS, Canada

Fabricator
Signworld

For this gift-shop and gallery sign, enamels were used to hand-paint the illustration and lettering. The double-sided sign measures 3 x 4 ft.

Designer
Lorel Marketing Group
E. Greenbush, NY

Fabricator
Saxton Sign Co.
Schodack, NY

This ceiling-mounted sign for a mall food court measures 4 x 17 ft. and includes stainless-steel skewered and fabricated letters, complete with exposed neon mounted on the letter faces. The pizza slice at right has push-through olives and pepperoni with polished edges. Both the burger and pizza slice are double-faced.

Designer
Sparky Potter
Wood & Wood Sign Co.
Waitsfield, VT

Fabricator
Wood & Wood Sign Co.

This 36 x 42-in. sign was fabricated from one mahogany slab. The letters were hand-carved and gilded. The logo was cut from 1/4-in. expanded plastic and painted a gloss red.

Designer
Chip Spirson
Vital Signs
Pensacola, FL

Fabricator
Vital Signs

This 8 x 4-ft. sign was carved from a single
1 1/2-in. thick sheet of composite board. The
background was smalted with crushed black
quartz. The letters are silver with silver gutters,
and the gold is 23K. There are no added pieces
or "glue-ons;" this sign is one solid piece with
deep carving and high relief.

Designer
Sparky Potter
Wood & Wood Sign Co.
Waitsfield, VT

Fabricator
Wood & Wood Sign Co.

The sign is approximately 3 ft. 6 in. x 2 ft. 4 in.
The front side illustration is woodburned, painted
with acrylics and housepaints and varnished. The
back side is painted with house paints. The illustration and design idea came from a Crabtree &
Evelyn catalog.

Designer
Gary Anderson
Bloomington Design
Bloomington, IN

Fabricator
Bloomington Design

This 18 x 24-in. flower-shop sign has sandblasted redwood with a latex finish. Lettering
was carved, rounded and gilded.

Designer
ARTeffects, Inc.
Bloomfield, CT

Fabricator
ARTeffects, Inc.

For this signage for a restaurant and night club, flexible faces were stretched over an iron framework. The frame was capped on the edges with aluminum and sprayed gold. The Picasso-esque artwork was rendered with lettering enamels. The sign cabinet below utilizes exposed ultra-blue argon to announce the club's name.

Designer
Willie Wells
Signworld
Bridgewater, NS, Canada

Fabricator
Signworld

For this gift-shop and gallery sign, enamels were used to hand-paint the illustration and lettering. The double-sided sign measures 3 x 4 ft.

Designer
Kraig Yaseen
Yaseen Design Studio
Durango, CO

Fabricator
Yaseen Design Studio

This double-sided sign measures approximately 20 x 27 in. The oval is sandblasted and the banner is "stacked" MDO for depth. The copy is 18K and 23K goldleaf.

Designer
Eric Kramer
Sign Consultants, Inc.
Minneapolis, MN

Fabricator
Back Bay Awning Company
Boston, MA

An internally-illuminated canopy enhances entry to this restaurant, while also adding height and significance to the building.
Overall measurements: 10 x 18 ft.

Designer
Mark Oatis
Smith, Nelson & Oatis

Fabricators
Smith, Nelson & Oatis
Denver, CO
Independent Sign Co.
Denver, CO

For this restaurant, the sign comprises an aluminum cabinet finished in enamels. The lighting is a combination of exposed neon and incandescent bulbs.

Designers
Susannah and Stephen Garrity
Garrity Carved Signs Co.
Belmont, MA

Fabricators
Garrity Carved Signs Co.
George Castonguay (custom-wrought iron)
W. Roxbury, MA

The full-dimension lion is 34 in. tall; it was made of laminated Honduran mahogany over a 1-in. steel rod. The lion's teeth and tongue are copper. The carving has several vapor barriers, is coated with a resin and gilded with 23K gold foil. The mast arm was made from 70-year-old, custom-wrought iron.

Designer
Kai Dawley
Dawley Carved Signs
Oak Bluffs, MA

Fabricator
Dawley Carved Signs

This double-sided sugar pine sign is 4 ft. in dia-meter. The pine sections were strategically glued up for the head, plate of muffins, and feet. The pictorial is relief-carved. The copy is incised and finished in 23K goldleaf.

Designer
Gary Anderson
Bloomington Design
Bloomington, IN

Fabricator
Bloomington Design

This 2 x 4-ft. hanging sign comprises enamel on MDO with a silk-screened pictorial. The sign was then glazed and given prismatic painted letters.

Designer
Angel Osorio
Art & Design
Oranjestad, Aruba, Dutch Caribbean

Fabricators
Spanjer Brothers, Inc.
Addison, IL
Art & Design (installation)
Carlos Dania Contractors (installation)
Oranjestad, Aruba, Dutch Caribbean

Measuring 28-in. wide x 13-ft. high, this sign comprises aluminum and acrylic lettering. It is internally illuminated by fluorescant lamps.

Designer
Gary Anderson
Bloomington Design
Bloomington, IN

Fabricator
Bloomington Design

This 16 x 36-in. gift-shop sign is sandblasted redwood finished in latex. The rose was carved from foam and then applied.

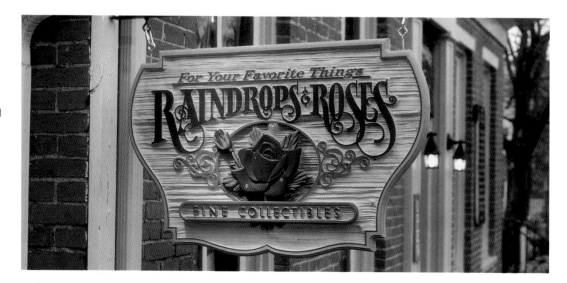

Designer
Marge Williams
Reno, NV

Fabricator
Federal Sign
Sparks, NV

This display is the entryway for the Las Vegas Casino in the Hyatt Atrium Hotel, Budapest, Hungary. The canopy was fabricated in gold-polished aluminum; the top and bottom tiers were bordered in blue, turquoise and gold neon. "Casino" is of open-channel construction, painted white. "Las Vegas" is reverse channel painted white. Copy overlay is green vinyl with exposed green neon. The revolving door entry was covered with a ribbed mirror polished bronze.

Designers
Joe Cusick, Noel Weber
Classic Sign Studio
Boise, ID

Fabricator
Classic Sign Studio

The circular sign for this coffee house measures 3 ft. in diameter, and was fabricated from high-density foam and composite board.

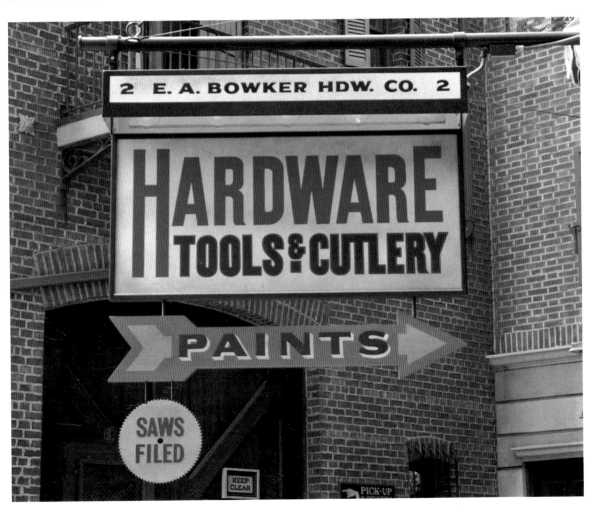

Designers
Sparky Potter
Wood & Wood Sign Co.
Waitsfield, VT
Universal Studios
Orlando, FL

Fabricator
Wood & Wood Sign Co.

The sign panels were constructed of composite board. The 5 x 3-ft. frame is mahogany. All lettering was laid out by hand and painted with latex house paints. The lighting canopy is fabricated metal and painted with enamels.

Designer
Ben McKnight
Sharper Images
Duluth, MN

Fabricator
Sharper Images

This sign, which identifies a multiple-shop mini-mall complex, was made of 2-in.-thick high-density foam. The 39-in.-diameter sign was sandblasted, leaving raised letters. The outer letters are leafed with black variegated goldleaf. "Shops" consists of raised letters with hand-carved prismatic faces gilded with 23K.

Designer
Glaser Associates, Inc.
Cincinnati, OH

Fabricator
Queen City Awning
Cincinnati, OH

Six double-faced sign assemblies identify a down-town retail office building. Measuring 7 1/2 x 5 1/2 ft., the signs were fabricated of .090 aluminum and 1-in. square tube steel.

Designer
Debbie Squires
Art Directions
Clearwater, FL

Fabricator
On Board Signs
Dunedin, FL

This hand-carved mahogany sign is for a jazz club in downtown St. Petersburg. It features goldleaf letters and artist's acrylics for the filagree.

Designer
Don Brewer
AMG Sign Company
Pittsburgh, PA

Fabricator
AMG Sign Company

This unit is fabricated with a 3 x 3-in. galvanized angle frame, a .090 aluminum face, and open channel letters and borders. The sign measures 12 ft. at the widest point and is 61 ft. high. A total of 3,172 11-watt lamps illuminate the surface with a flashing-chasing action.

Designer
Willie Wells
Signworld
Bridgewater, NS, Canada

Fabricator
Signworld

The 30 x 40-ft. double-sided sign was carved from mahogany; the gilded letters were outlined in black.

Designer
Lynda Najarian
Business Neon
San Francisco, CA

Fabricator
Neon Fabrications
Concord, CA

This double-sided sign comprises a 15-ft.-tall black metal cabinet with the client's name reaching toward the sky vertically and a horizontal neon hamburger to specify the nature of the business.

Designers
Neil True
ABCO Markets
Phoenix, AZ
Steve Kuipers
Christy Signs
Phoenix, AZ

Fabricator
Christy Signs

This metal sign (6 x 28 ft.) was painted with a thermo-copper coating and thermo-antique solution to achieve the patina copper appearance. Lighted, self-contained pan-channel letters were used to form "ABCO Foods"; the faces are of clear acrylic with two layers of peach-colored film. Letters were outlined with white neon. "Desert Market" and the cactus logo are sheetmetal reverse pan channels, backlit with turquoise neon.

Designer
Will Miller
Miller Signs
Glen Rock, NJ

Fabricator
Miller Signs

This double-sided, 2 1/2 x 3-ft. sign for the sign-maker's own shop was hand-carved from redwood with 23K gilded copy and bead molding. The panels are natural mahogany with a clear-coat finish. The block ornaments are clear-finished oak and the iron bracket is antique.

Designer
Gary Rhodes
Surfside Signs
Bellingham, WA

Fabricator
Surfside Signs

The gyro man for this boardwalk sandwich stand was hand-carved from high-density urethane. This figure sits on top of a steel frame that also supports the signs. All of the signs were hand-painted, as was the gyro man.

Designer
Ross Ireland
Cypress Carving Ltd.
N. Vancouver, BC, Canada

Fabricator
Cypress Carving Ltd.

Double-sided and made to look like a crate hanging from a crane, this sign measures 4 x 5 ft. The scoop was installed by the client.

Designer
Elton Hannaman
Hannaman Sign Crafters
Carlisle, PA

Fabricator
Hannaman Sign Crafters

Measuring 5 x 4 ft., this sign was constructed of 4 1/2-in.-thick laminated redwood. The letters were carved and gilded, as was the wreath.

Designer
Nickie Gorsky
Signcrafters
Nevada City, CA

Fabricator
Signcrafters

This 42 x 44-in. sign was textured and marbleized with enamels from 3-in.-thick pine. The statue was hand-painted. The main copy was scanned and the vinyl cut from original, handdrawn art. The entire sign was clear-coat finished.

Designer
Dan O'Brien
Udita Sparks (illustration)
The Rainbow-Dawn
Halifax, NS, Canada

Fabricator
The Rainbow-Dawn

Hand-carved in kiln-dried cedar, this hanging sign for a hotel/inn features "V"-cut incised letters with 23K goldleaf. The crest was carved in detail and applied.

Designer
David Ashton
David Ashton & Co., Ltd.
Baltimore, MD

Fabricator
Triangle Sign & Service
Baltimore, MD

The goal here was to provide unique period signage that would be the premiere graphic identification for the new major-league baseball park in Baltimore. The double-faced clock structure (14 ft. in diameter) exceeds 5500 pounds; each hand-painted scroll measures 9 x 9 ft.; the "Orioles" letters mounted atop the clock stand 36 in. high and have orange neon mounted to the face of each letter. For the Oriole-bird weather vanes, each ornithologically correct bird stands 8 ft. above the steel support structure on top of the scoreboard.

"The Logo Sun" illuminated letters were designed to duplicate the masthead logo of the Baltimore Sun newspaper. Each letter measures 6 ft. high with mounted white neon. The sun logo stands 6 ft. high and is 22 ft. long; the face was decorated with hand-cut vinyl copy.

More than 50 custom ad panels were constructed to mimick old-time roadside billboards. Illumination is provided by gooseneck lamps. To achieve an old-time effect, a custom fabricated extrusion surrounds the ad copy area; welded aluminum bar stock was used to create the cross-hatch effect at the bottom of each panel.

The park entrance signs stand 42 in. tall and are of high-prismatic, stainless steel. Each letter was built by hand and then installed on an existing steel support structure above the main entrance to the stadium.

Photo courtesy of Rick North

Designer
Peter Poanessa
Walpole, NH

Fabricator
Peter Poanessa

This 2 ft. x 3 ft. x 2-in. sign is genuine mahogany. The illustration was relief-carved, the lettering incised. Soft colors and clear finish keep the feel of the theme of the bookstore.

Designer
Uxbridge Carvers
Uxbridge, MA

Fabricator
Uxbridge Carvers

The 3 x 5-ft. double-sided sign was carved from redwood, and the pictorial was hand-painted.

Designer
Sparky Potter
Wood & Wood Signs
Waitsfield, VT

Fabricator
Wood & Wood Signs

Given an extremely windy location, the designer created an airy sign. The main slabs were laminated with a combination of house paints with acrylic artist panels, clear-coated with spar varnish. The lettering was hand-carved and gilded. The ribbons were carved in foam, the utensils in mahogany. Knife, fork and spoon were then gilded as well.

Designer
Fox-Suarez Signs
Decatur, TX

Fabricator
Fox-Suarez Signs

This 15 x 20-in., double-faced sign is 1 3/4 in. thick with 1/4-in. frosted glass. The main copy was routed and then gilded with 23K gold.

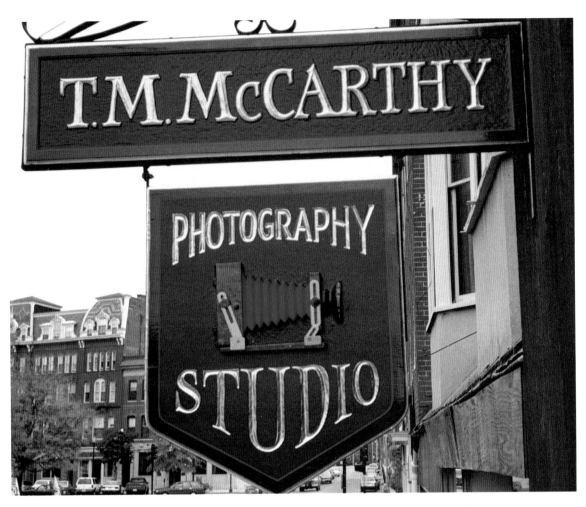

Designer
Peter Poanessa
Signwright
Walpole, NH

Fabricator
Signwright

Two-in. mahogany with 1/4-in. flat steel bracket the entirety of this sign. The camera is an exact copy of an antique owned by the client.

Designer
Neon Products Ltd.
Vancouver, BC, Canada

Fabricator
Neon Products Ltd.

This double-faced sign measuring 3 x 4 ft. utilizes exposed neon.

Designer
Ann Nelson
Vineyard Haven, MA

Fabricator
Dawley Carved Signs
Oak Bluffs, MA

Made of 3-in.-thick Honduras mahogany
(4 1/2 ft. in diameter), this relief carving of
grapes and leaves was painted with acrylics.
The copy was incised, carved and finished in
23K goldleaf. The quill bracket is fabricated
steel, and gilded.

Designer
Douglas Williams
Douglas Williams Woodcarving
Honolulu, HI

Fabricator
Douglas Williams Woodcarving

This 3 x 2 1/2-ft., double-sided sign was carved
from high-density foam. The graphics were hand-
painted. The horizontal piece was carved from
koa wood.

Designer
Gregory Beck
Otter Creek Industries Inc.
Middlebury, VT

Fabricators
Otter Creek Industries Inc.
Forster
Victor, NY
Graphitek of Vermont, Inc.
Bennington, VT

For this Mexican fast-food restaurant, four box-shaped awnings were combined with a shaped cactus to form the framework for the fabric and graphic work. The latter combined welded framework with vinyl-applied graphics and lettering.

Designer
Gary Anderson
Bloomington Design
Bloomington, IN

Fabricator
Bloomington Design

This 24 x 28-in. MDO sign was done with enamels and abalone shell accents.

Designer
Larry Garcia Smith
Heath Sign Co.
Portland, OR

Fabricator
Heath Sign Co.

Commissioned by the Portland Trailblazers, an NBA franchise, this 5-ft. diameter sphere was fabricated of spun aluminum. "Blazers" was formed, embossed and pushed through the routed aluminum background. "On Broadway" was painted black with routing to effect marquee lights.

Designers
Mark Oatis, Rufus Desoto
Smith, Nelson & Oatis
Denver, CO

Fabricators
Smith, Nelson & Oatis
Independent Sign Co. (metal work)
Denver, CO

This sign for a gaming hall has a 1/8-in. aluminum, pan-channel panel. Automotive sign enamels and green glass smalts were used for the finish; 23K goldleaf and 10K white gold decorate carved and PVC letters. The channel letters are 23K gold.

POLE- OR POST-MOUNTED SIGNS

Post- or pole-mounted signs are yet another type of free-standing sign, but exclusive by the exposed poles or post structures to which their respective sign faces are mounted. The best examples integrate posts or poles with the other facets of the sign's design, reflecting complementary choices of materials, colors, shapes, etc.

Designer
Andy Bellina
Brecksville, OH

Fabricator
Andy Bellina

The double-faced entry sign for a public swimming area stands 9 ft. high and 19 ft. wide. The 6-ft.-diameter mill stone and the cut quarry-rock planter were excavated from the abandoned quarry that was filled to make the swimming area. The tongue and mortised 12 x 12-in. cedar beams are hand-cut and sandblasted to give an aged look; everything is finished with a water seal. Trees and shrubs planted coincide with a landscaping mandate for natural material.

Designer
Daniel Dillon
Dillon Design Associates
Cohoes, NY

Fabricator
Dillon Design Associates

This double-sided 4 x 3-ft., laminated, composite board sign was hand-carved and gilded with 23K goldleaf copy. The raised flourish and ram heads were custom fabricated from high-density urethane. The sign panel is supported by 4 x 4-in. raised panel posts with caps.

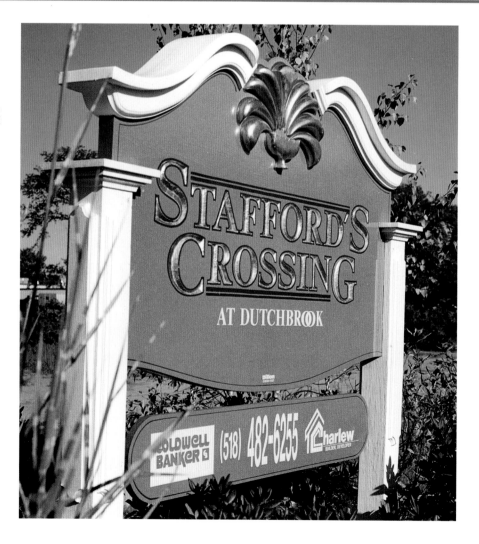

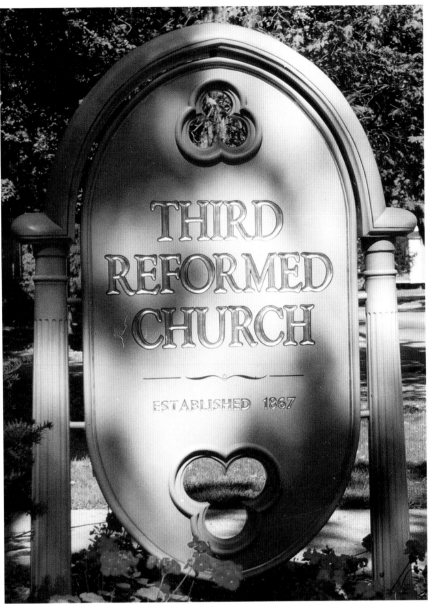

Designers
Bob Krause
Bob Krause Wood Graphics
Douglas, MI
Mark Bonnette
Holland, MI

Fabricator
Bob Krause Wood Graphics

This double-faced 3 x 5-ft. sign incorporates a 2-in.-thick piece of high-density urethane and an additional 3/4-in.-thick piece for the raised borders. The crown on top was fabricated from three 2-in. pieces of the urethane glued together. The hand-shaped posts were purchased from a lumber yard. Hollow basswood and cedar posts were installed inside and stuck in the ground. The sign was hand-carved, and the lettering was gilded. The outline and striping is maroon.

Designer
Will Miller
Miller Signs
Glen Rock, NJ

Fabricators
Miller Signs
A & F Sign Co. (installation)
Paterson, NJ

This 48 x 78 x 2-in. sign was created from redwood. The elliptical panel was gilded, and the main copy was hand-carved. The dogwood blossoms were hand-hammered from copper (detailed with antiqued paint). Four-in. spun-brass finals top the 4 x 4-in. milled and routed cornerposts.

Designer
Sign Consultants, Inc.
Minneapolis, MN

Fabricator
Signcrafters Outdoor Display Inc.
Fridley, MN

This sign features an internally-illuminated cabinet with routed faces and vinyl stripe detail. The exposed neon border detail is repetitive of the architectural detail.

Designer
The Design Works
Vancouver, BC, Canada

Fabricator
Imperial Sign Corporation
Port Coquitlam, BC, Canada

Created for a food court and retail businesses in a waterfront mall, this sign measures 6 1/2 x 11 ft. with a 3 x 6-ft. mid section. The top portion was constructed entirely of aluminum, with 16-gauge perforated sides and top, and 1/8-in. linear perforated faces, allowing neon light to emit. The mid section is elliptical with routed copy backed with acrylic. Decorative nautical trim completes the sail look.

Designer
Brian Kurzius
Adirondack Sign & Design
Saranac Lake, NY

Fabricator
Adirondack Sign & Design

This 8 ft. x 19-in. sign has an MDO plywood background. The border is raised pine with molding and a gilded, routed outline. The letters were carved from high-density urethane and gilded. The dark brown outline was painted directly on the background. The caps on the post are high-density urethane with 23K gold.

Designer
Sparky Potter
Wood & Wood Sign Co.
Waitsfield, VT

Fabricator
Wood & Wood Sign Co.

This double-faced sign for a construction company is 5 x 4 ft. The woodburned gnome illustration was painted and finish-coated with varnish.

Designer
Paul Bentsen
Bentsen Signs
E. Greenwich, RI

Fabricator
Bentsen Signs

This 4 x 6-ft. sign combines redwood and mahogany with goldleaf. The cow's face is 3D. The "quilted-look" border uses corn. Tim Jansen is the name of the current tenant farmer, and that plaque is removable. The post-and-beam effect was created with full-mortise cross beams.

Designers
David and Laura Maine
MaineLine Graphics
Deering, NH

Fabricator
MaineLine Graphics

In German, "Steinhorst" means "nest in the crack of the rock." This 54 x 60-in. single-face sign was sandblasted and hand-carved from 8/4 redwood. The graphics are 23K goldleaf and enamel paint. The eagle, nest and eaglets were hand-carved from 5/4 redwood and glued on to the 8/4 redwood sign face. These items were then airbrushed and painted with enamels. The posts are rock-face granite.

Designer
Roger Sherman Partners, Inc.
Dearborn, MI

Fabricator
Planet Neon Signs & Lighting
Novi, MI

Wooly Bully's restaurant exudes a 1950s and '60s atmosphere, including a displayed collection of classic guitars. To compliment the collection, this 9 x 30-ft., double-faced guitar was constructed of aluminum, each side with more than 300 ft. of exposed neon (strings, outlines and letters). The guitar is complete in every detail, down to the "Gibson" trademark and "Les Paul" signature. Internal angle-iron framing and a single, 14-in.-diameter pole support the cantilevered installation with a concrete footing.

Designer
Elton Hannaman
Hannaman Sign Crafters
Carlisle, PA

Fabricator
Hannaman Sign Crafters

This 3 x 4-ft. sign for a restaurant was made from 1-in. redwood and features hand-carved letters. Some portions of the sign were gilded, and other were hand-painted.

Designer
Gary Anderson
Bloomington Design
Bloomington, IN

Fabricator
Bloomington Design

This floral-shop flower was carved from foam and hand-painted with acrylic latex. The main sign is 6 x 8-ft. MDO board. The lettering is vinyl; the frame is cedar.

Designer
Edward Manning
Gemini Sign & Design Ltd.
Conway, NH

Fabricator
Gemini Sign & Design Ltd.

This 4 x 7-ft. painted MDO sign has airbrushed artwork and cut-out MDO letters. The posts are 4 x 6 in.

Designers
Kevin Mills, Todd Hanson, Noel Weber
Classic Sign Studio
Boise, ID

Fabricator
Classic Sign Studio

The center panel spans 5 x 18 ft. The ribbon and the brush tips were fabricated from high-density urethane. The chisels have mahogany handles; the blades are polished aluminum. The background is marbled, wood composite board, as are the wings and letters. The edge is gilded, and the background is blue smalts.

Designers
Anthony Field
N. Vancouver, BC, Canada
Karen Reithofer
John Peachey & Associates
N. Vancouver, BC, Canada

Fabricators
John Peachey & Associates
Frank Corius (carving)
N. Vancouver, BC, Canada

This sign has multi-level, three-dimensional graphics. The leaves, lettering and masks are hand-carved, hand-painted, high-density foam. The violin is carved mahogany; the paint pallet and brush are cedar. Steel brackets were used for mounting above the roof line. Overall size is 13 ft. x 50 in.

Designer
Signage, Inc.
Marysville, WA

Fabricator
Signage, Inc.

This sign comprises custom fabricated sheetmetal for the cabinet, custom full-round sugar pine letters with 23K goldleaf finish. Overall size is approximately 4-ft. high x 19-ft. to the point.

Designers
Stephen Sutton, Bill Shaw
New England Sign Carvers
Middlefield, CT

Fabricator
New England Sign Carvers

This 76 x 23-in. mahogany sign features hand-carved letters with 23K goldleaf.

Designer
Barb Schoos
John Luttmann, Woodcarver
Phoenixville, PA

Fabricator
John Luttmann, Woodcarver

Fabricated of South American mahogany, this sign measures 35 x 48 x 3 in. "The Cricket Corner" was hand-carved and gilded with 23K goldleaf. The cricket logo and "gift gallery" are flat 23K goldleaf on a raised panel.

Designer
Don Brewer
AMG Sign Company
Pittsburgh, PA

Fabricator
AMG Sign Company

This free-standing sign was designed using existing corporate graphics to identify an office in a progressively-styled building. Fabricated with an extruded aluminum cabinet and rectangular aluminum upright cladding, the sign faces measure 6 x 7 ft.

Designer
Daniel Dillon
Dillon Design Associates
Cohoes, NY

Fabricators
Dillon Design Associates
Schrader and Co., Inc.
Burnt Hills, NY

This double-faced, 5 x 9-ft. carved redwood sign includes custom-milled rams' heads fabricated from redwood. The "850" is a raised 5/4 redwood panel with 23K gold-filled letters and a marbleized background. The flourish on the bottom of the sign was hand-carved from 5/4 redwood. "Schrader and Company" was hand-carved; "Professional Remodeling . . ." was flat painted. The pillars were custom-milled and fabricated from poplar and a wood composite. The sign reflects the type of work that the client can provide.

Designer
Chip Spirson
Vital Signs
Pensacola, FL

Fabricator
Vital Signs

This sign identifies a restored Victorian house that was transformed into a law office. Measuring approximately 4 x 3 ft., the sign's blank lower area is reserved for the name of a second attorney. Each face of the double-sided sign has a different color scheme that reflects its Florida location.

Designer
Openwood Studios Inc.
Madison, WI

Fabricator
Openwood Studios Inc.

Commissioned by the City of Fitchburg, Wisconsin to illustrate Fitchburg's agricultural history, this sign measures 12 x 5 ft. It was sandblasted from clear, vertical grain redwood.

Designers
Bob Hedrick, Ann Hubbard, Chris Wisemen
Cornoyer-Hedrick
Phoenix, AZ

Fabricator
SmithCraft Mfg. Co., Inc.

This logo represents the flight of a tennis ball. The "flight" structure is fabricated aluminum, 17 1/2 ft. high; the tennis ball is a 2-ft., perforated aluminum ball with internal neon. To diffuse the neon's glare and conform to local codes, a matte-finished, high-impact polycarbonate was placed in front of the neon.

Photo courtesy of Rick North

Designer
Ivan Solomon
Creative Thinker Inc.
Vancouver, BC, Canada

Fabricator
Ireland, Peachey & Company
N. Vancouver, BC, Canada

This routed cedar sign fixed on cedar posts measures 4 x 8 ft.

Designer
Dwayne E. Freeby
Freeby Studios
Johns Island, SC

Fabricator
Freeby Studios

Overall sign is 10 ft. x 5 ft. 3 in. The hand-laminated post is 3 1/2 x 6 in. x 35 ft. The plywood sign is boxed with ceramic tile. The double-faced, sandblasted 1-in.-thick logo (Indian design furnished) is epoxy-bronzed and gilded. The tile is terra cotta. Riders are sandblasted red cedar. The lettering is wheat colored.

Designer
Sparky Potter
Wood & Wood Sign Co.
Waitsfield, VT

Fabricator
Wood & Wood Sign Co.

This 3 x 5-ft. pine slab sign face is framed in butternut. The woodburned image was painted and finish-coated with varnish.

Designers
Gary Stamper, Denise Bartlett
Sign Service Co.
Hayden Lake, ID

Fabricator
Sign Service Co.

This 8 x 8-ft. mounted sign with a polished copper cabinet contains exposed neon mounted inside and open pan channel letters outside. These were mounted to 1/2-in. thick clear acrylic, with a black background and backlit blue grid. The broken tile mosaic is on yet another level and is mounted on MDO.

Designer
David Showalter
David Design
Bryan, OH

Fabricator
David Design

This 6 x 4-ft. redwood sign was mounted on cedar posts and painted white with latex. The logo and lettering were done with enamels; the heart and sun were stage-blasted for a cross line effect.

Designers
Noel Weber, Kevin Mills, Todd Hanson
Classic Sign Studio
Boise, ID

Fabricator
Classic Sign Studio

The letters were made from cut-out foam, while the shamrock is vinyl. Each of these features was sprayed over.

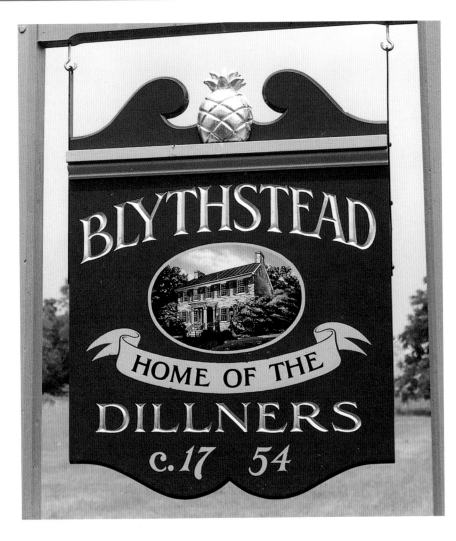

Designer
Elton Hannaman
Hannaman Sign Crafters
Carlisle, PA

Fabricator
Hannaman Sign Crafters

This double-faced sign for a private residence measures 28 x 31 in. The sign was carved from 1-in. redwood. The copy is hand-carved and gilded with 23K gold, as was the pineapple application. The pictorial was hand-painted from a photograph of the Dillner's house.

Designer
Jon Wanbaugh
Outdoor Dimensions
Anaheim, CA

Fabricator
Outdoor Dimensions

This is a box design with an asymmetrical rod iron accent. The copy was sandblasted and painted; the logo is a cut-out, hand-painted applique.

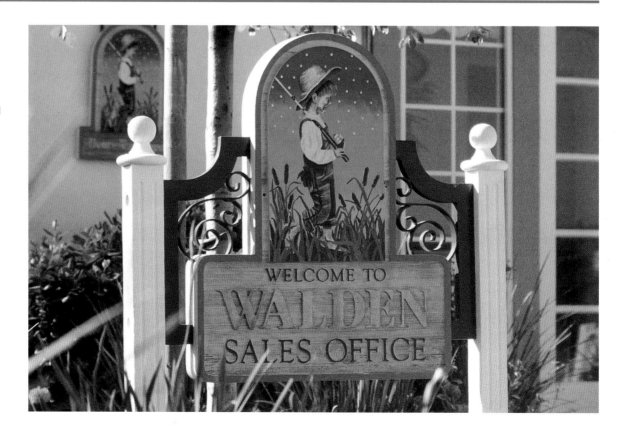

Designers
Bill Pierson
Pierson Building Center
Eureka, CA
Neale Penfold
Penfold Civil Engineering
Eureka, CA
Dave Duda
Mercury Neon
Eureka, CA

Fabricators
Mercury Neon
NCI Inc.
Eureka, CA
McHale's Sign Service
Redding, CA

"The Big Hammer" was created for a building center and lumber yard. Standing 26-ft. tall, the hammer has a steel tube core, a solid wood handle, a painted sheet-steel cabinet and a brushed, stainless-sheet steel head. The sign itself comprises red channel letters and clear plastic faces with a red trim cap. The white plastic reader board incorporates exposed 12mm ruby neon ("At the Big Hammer"). Two ivory sign cabinets were attached to the core pole with painted sheetmetal gusset to finish the one-piece, sign-cabinet look.

Designer
Ken Siegrist
Coast Graphics & Signs, Inc.
Stafford, TX
Fabricator
Coast Graphics & Signs, Inc.

Measuring 12 x 12, this sign is fabricated of aluminum. "Coast" is made of flexible vinyl. The palm trees have green outline neon. "Graphics+" is open-faced channel. "Signs" is regular channel with plastic faces. Overall height is 35 ft.

Designer
Ross Ireland
Ireland, Peachey & Company
N. Vancouver, BC, Canada
Fabricator
Ireland, Peachey & Company

This carved cedar sign features gilded lettering.

Designer
Nancy Bennett
Dannco
Centerville, IA

Fabricator
Dannco

This antiques-and-crafts shop sign has a single sheet of 1/2-in. MDO plywood that was flush-mounted on sturdy posts. All graphics and lettering were painted by hand. The emerald-hook "plaque" was hand-marbled to appear three-dimensional.

Designer
Steven L. Miller
Signworks Design & Production, Inc.
Lakeworth, FL

Fabricator
Signworks Design & Production, Inc.

Except for the cap, this sign was fabricated from 3-in. high-density foam, then attached to a 6 x 6-in. post using solid aluminum bars. The copy and the cat are in relief. The sign was finished with a clear satin coat to protect the colors.

Designer
Billy Williamson
Stonegraphics
Tyler, TX

Fabricator
Stonegraphics

Laminated redwood and a sand sculpturing process produced this sign.

Designers
Bob DeRobbio
Newport Beach, CA
Paul DeRobbio
Garden Grove, CA

Fabricator
Expressions Advertising
Anaheim, CA

This sign is 27 ft. high and 15 ft. wide. The tower roofs are made of .060 sheet copper to match towers on the building. The tower windows are leaded glass and are illuminated by 4500 white neon. The towers themselves are fabricated of sheetmetal. The main sign body is .090 alumi-num over a steel frame; the copy is individually-illuminated channel letters.

Designer
William Cochran
The Signworks
Walkersville, MD

Fabricator
The Signworks

The sign and frame are wood with beveled edges, channels and embellishments. The background was stippled to give a lighter "halo" around the carved wheat, which was painted gold with umber glaze. The lettering was painted gold with dark red shadows. The sign is freeswinging inside the frame, which is post-channeled and chamfered and set in brick.

Designers
Abadh Whiteway, Dan O'Brien
The Rainbow-Dawn
Halifax, NS, Canada

Fabricator
The Rainbow-Dawn

Hand-carved in kiln-dried cedar, this 4 1/2 x 6-ft. sign for a pewtersmith features "V"-cut lettering in classic style. The graphic was hand-carved from a main sign blank depicting the owner at work.

ENTRY MONUMENTS

Entry monuments are a special type of ground sign, separated from their counterparts by their conspicuous size and their distance from the complexes whose presence they announce. A relatively new addition to the field of sign design, the entry monument was developed in response to the specific needs of such end users as industrial parks and large residential projects.

Designer
PETERHANSREA
Birmingham, MI

Fabricator
Planet Neon Signs & Lighting
Novi, MI

This 12-ft.-tall sign is all fabricated metal. The numerals were made from .063 fabricated aluminum and stand 40 in. high. The pylons are 12-ft.-tall fabricated steel pipe. The entire sign has a metallic paint finish.

Designer
Gary Bell
Don Bell & Company
Port Orange, FL

Fabricator
Don Bell & Company

This single-faced cedar sign has a sandblasted background, raised copy and logo. The sign is mounted between various cedar wood posts and is illuminated externally by floodlights.

Designer
Luttmann Brothers Woodcarving & Sign Co.
Phoenixville, PA

Fabricator
Luttmann Brothers Woodcarving & Sign Co.

Fabricated from mahogany, two such 33 x 9-ft. signs mark the entrance of a residential development. The thistles were carved from 2-in. maho-gany and then applied before priming and painting.

Designer
Mike Osburn
Anderson Debartolo Pan
Tucson, AZ

Fabricator
Signtific Signs
Tucson, AZ

This sign is an architectural brick structure with brass letters painted to match the cast bronze logo. The letters are mounted on a metal insert and backlighted with white neon. Overall size: 2 x 10 ft.

Designer
Communication Arts
Boulder, CO

Fabricator
Gordon Sign Company
Denver, CO

The four faces of this sign are made of .125 aluminum attached directly to the exposed space frame. The north and south faces measure 5 x 25 ft.

Designer
Thomas J. Dever
Luttmann Brothers Woodcarving & Sign Co.
Phoenixville, PA

Fabricator
Luttmann Brothers Woodcarving & Sign Co.

Two such signs attract the attention of drivers from the highway to a shopping center. Laminated South American mahogany comprises both signs, which are bent to a 10-degree radius along a wall. The panels measure 36 x 9 ft. and are mounted to a 48 x 9 1/2-ft. foam panel attached to the brick wall.

Designer
Woodmark
Akron, OH

Fabricator
Woodmark

This entrance sign comprises three laminated Douglas Fir panels on a brick structure that matches the buildings on the site. The logo panels are 3 x 10 ft. x 5-in. thick. The address panel is 2 ft. wide. Both are finished with semi-transparent oil stain. The brick structure, which also encloses electrical equipment, is 3 x 14 x 6 ft.

Designer
ARTeffects, Inc.
Bloomfield, CT

Fabricator
ARTeffects, Inc.

For this signage for a restaurant and night club, flexible faces were stretched over an iron framework. The frame was capped on the edges with aluminum and sprayed gold. The Picasso-esque artwork was rendered with lettering enamels. The sign cabinet below utilizes exposed ultra-blue argon to announce the club's name.

Designer
Mark Wygonik
Image Maker's Ink
Vero Beach, FL

Fabricator
Curt Oxford Woodcarver, Inc.
Sebastian, FL

Overall length is 12 ft. for this sandblasted redwood sign with redwood cut-out letters. The steamboat pictorial was hand-painted. Wrought iron decorates the sides and the backdrop is rough-sawn cedar.

Designer
Merv Eckman
Adcon Inc.
Ft. Collins, CO

Fabricator
Adcon Inc.

Pan channel letters on cedar tongue-and-groove wood, masonry and steel make up this sign for an office park. The logo is stained glass with a polycarbonate cover.

Designer
David Hornblow
The Sign Works
Vancouver, BC, Canada

Fabricator
Shakespeare Signs
Surrey, BC, Canada

This double-pole mounted sign is of steel and concrete fabrication.

Designer
Merv Eckman
Adcon Signs
Ft. Collins, CO

Fabricator
Adcon Signs

This sign is constructed of .125 welded steel with 1/2-in.-thick PVC letters with a polyurethane finish. The base is artificial stone.

Designer
Envirographics, Inc.
Orlando, FL

Fabricator
Envirographics, Inc.

This sign is one of two 12-ft.-high concrete walls. The carriage lamps and graphics are polished brass.

Designer
Ivey, Bennett, Harris & Walls
Orlando, FL

Fabricator
Envirographics, Inc.
Orlando, FL

This 8 x 16 x 2-ft. entrance sign identifies a 164-acre high-tech business park at Kennedy Space Center. The cabinet is covered with aluminum-clad board and has a textured finish. Radiused ends are rolled in #4 brushed stainless steel. Graphics are reverse channel neon fabricated in aluminum and have an acrylic urethane enamel graduated paint finish.

Designers
Curtis Arbaugh, Forest Stiltner
Gable Signs & Graphics, Inc.
Baltimore, MD

Fabricators
Gable Signs & Graphics, Inc.
Tom Sappington Masonry (brick wall)
Baltimore, MD

The letters on the lower redwood panel features were hand-carved (incised). The upper-panel horn was hand-carved redwood, and it was applied on top of the half-circle redwood panel. Both panels have beveled edges.

Designer
Luttmann Brothers Woodcarving & Sign Co.
Phoenixville, PA

Fabricator
Luttmann Brothers Woodcarving & Sign Co.

This sign board is 18 in. x 7 ft. 9 in. x 1 1/4 in., bent laminated into a 6-ft. radius corresponding to the stone wall. The board is a lamination of five 1/4-in. layers of basswood. The lettering was hand-carved; the border was routed; and both are 23K goldleaf. The single-faced pheasant was carved out of basswood with the grain direction and joinery combined so that the grain runs with each long and thin element for strength. It was filled, coated with epoxy and illustrated with lettering enamels.

Designer
Dick Hendrickson
Cloquet, MN

Fabricator
Ins-Tent Manufacturing Company
Cloquet, MN

This sign was designed with an aluminum frame and an inner cage to slip over the goal post supports. A 4-ft. radius on both adds interest to this internally-lit sign. The finished size is 12 x 17 x 4 ft.

Designer
Mark Taylor
Natural Graphics, Inc.
Houston, TX

Fabricator
Natural Graphics, Inc.

This etched and in-filled sandstone sign is 10 ft. wide x 4 ft. 4 in. high and represents an identity upgrade for a renovated apartment community. The logos are cut-out and applied metal pieces, and they match the cap accent band.

Designers
ARTeffects, Inc.
Bloomfield, CT
New England Design
Mansfield, CT
Foxwoods Casino
Ledyard, CT

Fabricator
ARTeffects, Inc.

This wall-mounted sign is fabricated aluminum with halo letters mounted on a fabricated aluminum diamond. All finishes are teal acrylic lacquer and all halos are purple argon. Planter-mounted signs were sandblasted, edge-lit glass with a concealed fluorescent light source.

Designers
Stephens, Inc. (logo)
Grand Rapids, MI
Bruce Janssen (sign design)
The Wood Shop
Boyne City, MI

Fabricator
The Wood Shop

This sandblasted sign is 13 x 3 ft. and made from 8-in.-thick redwood. The 1 1/2-in. letters were cut-out from high-density urethane as was the cat. The cat's structure began with a welded steel-tube frame. The sculpted and carved urethane was finished with an acrylic enamel. The sign embodies the company's slogan: "Stalking the cat."

Designer
Michael Kinnunen
TubeArt
Seattle, WA

Fabricator
TubeArt

This 20 x 10 1/2-ft. monument ground sign was constructed of concrete. The reverse pan channel, halo-lit letters are fabricated sheetmetal with a painted green marble finish. The bars are solid brass, mounted in front of an internally-illuminated recessed area.

Designer
Merv Eckman
Adcon Inc.
Ft. Collins, CO

Fabricator
Adcon Inc.

This sign for the First Christian Church utilizes 1/8-in. steel plate in the cone with a texture finish. The ring is 1/2 x 12-in. steel.

Designers
John Steinberg
Artsign Design
Boise, ID
Eagle Landscape Nursery
Boise, ID

Fabricators
Artsign Design
Eagle Landscape Nursery

This 15 x 4-ft., painted composite board sign has cut-out overlays totaling four layers. The masonry and landscaping were designed to enhance the sign and entryway for a new home subdivision.

Designer
Ireland & Peachey
N. Vancouver, BC, Canada

Fabricator
Ireland & Peachey

Pin-mounted on a rock wall, this sign for a townhouse community features individually cut aluminum letters, and a routed, infilled waterfall.

Designers
Per Jacobsen, David Hornblow
The Design Works
Vancouver, BC, Canada

Fabricator
Shakespeare Signs
Surrey, BC, Canada

This sign is fabricated of painted steel, with a chromed logo facia and a granite base.

Sign Systems

Sign systems, or environmental graphics as they are often called by the design community, are collections of individual signs designed to identify and direct traffic to and/or through a complex or group of buildings. More often than not, a variety of sign types—hanging or projecting, wall-mounted or facia, ground or post-mounted—are utilized, but all of which work as a "system" based on common design elements, including materials, shapes, color, etc.

Designers
David M. Harding
A Sign of Excellence
Carrollton, TX
Tom Bolin
Bolin Masonry
Keller, TX

Fabricators
A Sign of Excellence
Bolin Masonry
Metro Metal Fabricators, Inc.
Dallas, TX

For this apartment complex, the main ID sign is approximately 76 x 96 in. at its base, with an internal steel frame to support the floating, triple-corbel brick arch. Sign faces were made from sandblasted redwood.

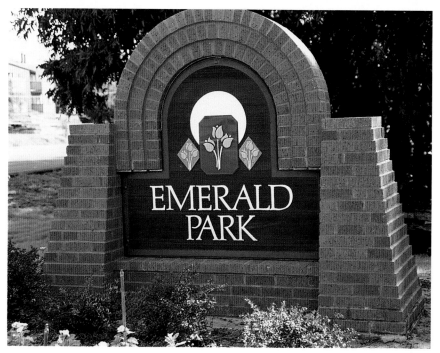

Designer
Mark Taylor
Natural Graphics, Inc.
Houston, TX

Fabricator
Natural Graphics, Inc.

The signage for this apartment community is a 64 x 76-in. section of redwood applied to a stucco structure. The copy and logo were sand-blasted and in-filled, and the sign was accented with a red-trim piece. The latter is carried throughout the sign system.

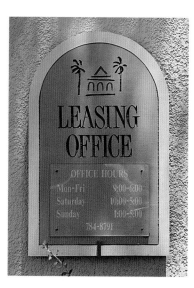

Designer
Brechin Morgan
Morgan Sign Co.
Norwalk, CT

Fabricator
Morgan Sign Co.

The agency wanted to brighten up a vacant, city-owned buidling until a developer could be found. In all, the 29 panels were painted in acrylic on plywood and set into window and door openings. Sizes range from 3 x 5 ft. to 8 x 10 ft. The focus is the industrial history of the area. The window artwork won the additional honor of being selected by Washington D.C.'s Urban Land Institute for inclusion in its 1993 appointment calendar.

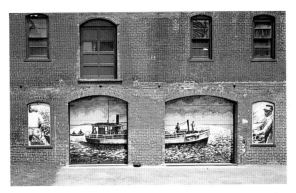

Designer
Terry Beier
Cornoyer-Hedrick
Phoenix, AZ

Fabricator
SmithCraft Mfg. Co., Inc.
Phoenix, AZ

The project team was commissioned to create a system of signs and pedestrian directories for the Fifth Ave. Arts District in Scottsdale, AZ. The free-standing signs are placed at major street boundaries of this district. The logo — a series of fabricated aluminum pans backed with neon — was created to reflect the Southwestern flavor of the area. The center element is fabricated from polished stainless steel.

Designer
Degnen Associates Inc.
Columbus, OH

Fabricator
Columbus Sign Co.
Columbus, OH

This civic system identifies an exposition that celebrates the 500th anniversary of its namesake Christopher Columbus's discovery of the New World. Each of these signs identifies a garden or entertainment venue. Sizes range from a 3-ft. diameter to a 3 x 4-ft. double-faced, sandblasted sign with redwood graphics and material pennants and ornamentation.

Designers
Bob Dail, Jeff Harley
Oklahoma Sign Co., Inc.
Tulsa, OK

Fabricator
Oklahoma Sign Co., Inc.

For Hastings, a retail store chain that sells books, music, etc., each sign averages approximately 54 x 72 in. Many of the signs incorporate neon (12mm) and layered transparent plastic mounted onto wooden grids. Most of the neon used behind the acrylic is white.

Designer
Rick Becker
Becker & Associates
Seattle, WA

Fabricator
Trade-Marx Sign & Display
Seattle, WA

The sign system for the Seattle Design Center consists of front signage and directories of aluminum construction, and elevator signs of aluminum and polycarbonate.

Designers
Mark Oatis (all except Bullwhackers and Bull Durham)
Todd Hoffman (Bull Durham)
Jim Schultz (Wild Card)
Smith, Nelson & Oatis
Denver, CO
Bright & Assoc. (Bullwhackers)
Venice, CA
Bill Hueg (Bull Durham, Womack's)
St. Paul, MN
Tri-Ad Adv. (Diamond Lil's)
Rapid City, SD
Dale Cody (Womack's)
Denver, CO
Brian King (Turf Club)
Cripple Creek, CO

Fabricators
Smith, Nelson & Oatis (all signs)
Independent Sign Co. (all except Diamond Lil's)
Denver, CO
Fantasy-in-Iron (all except Bullwhackers and Diamond Lil's)
Denver, CO

Each sign shares a common denominator of a fabricated aluminum background. Other common elements include 23K gold, lettering enamels and raised elements carved from PVC. Womack's and Bull Durham feature pictorials rendered in oils; Eureka! has a smalts background. The rope bracket in Bullwhackers was made of steel and cast fiberglass.

Designers
Constance Hesse Wicks, Cheryl Long O'Donnell, Richard M. Lang
VISUAL Communications
St. Paul, MN

Fabricators
SignArt
Eau Claire, WI
GlassArt Design
Minneapolis, MN
CoSigns
Minneapolis, MN

Two 2 x 10-ft. fabricated and etched aluminum "banner" signs identify the office tower entrance. Fifteen glass interior signs provide direction with first surface silkscreen and vinyl graphics. The background "spray" is matte in compliance with ADA, complementing the high gloss finish of the glass.

Designer
John Van Dyke
Van Dyke Co.
Seattle, WA

Fabricator
Trade-Marx Sign & Display
Seattle, WA

All of the signs were fabricated from 3/16-in. copper plate. The large one features reverse-cut letters, while the smaller ones have vinyl graphics.

Designer
Rauh, Good, Darlo & Barnes
Los Gatos, CA

Fabricator
Surfside Signs
Bellingham, WA

This system includes hand-painted walls and a grain silo, 23K gold windows with 18K gold centers and hand-carved restroom signs. The glass logo was sandblasted, acid-etched and glue-chipped. The other logo is hand-carved and sand-blasted mahogany.

Designer
Sparky Potter
Wood & Wood Sign Co.
Waitsfield, VT

Fabricator
Wood & Wood Sign Co.

All sign panels are fabricated of MDO with a combination of hand-painted and vinyl lettering. The burgees are cut-out of MDO and mounted off-surface for shadow and relief.

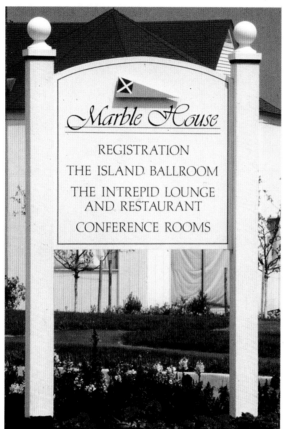

Designers
Mark Oatis, Jim Schultz
Smith, Nelson & Oatis
Denver, CO
RTKL Associates, Inc.
Baltimore, MD

Fabricator
Smith, Nelson & Oatis

Depicting different types of fare offered in a shopping mall food court, these five figures are each about 5 ft. tall. One is a metal "directional" figure, pointing the way to "Boulevard Cafes." The fully dimensional figures were built of a foam material.

Designers
Joe Mozdzen
On the Edge Design
Newport Beach, CA
Lisa Harrison
Harrison Design
Sherman Oaks, CA

Fabricators
Interstate Neon Co.
Van Nuys, CA
Cecil Sellers
Van Nuys, CA

All of these stores are part of a campus mall. Each sign has a seven-layer construction: a 1/16-in. backing of perforated metal painted yellow; a 1/4-in. cut-out, rusted steel plate; corrugated galvanized steel; painted PVC pipe; two separate layers of 1/2-in. cut-out, painted MDO plywood; and a top layer of hand-painted (or cut-out and painted) 1/2-in. MDO plywood. The exception is the 8 x 8-ft. "M" logo, which was fabricated from 1/4-in. rusted steel.

 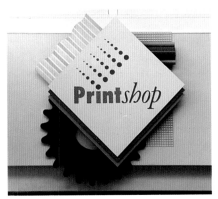

Designer

Shaughnessy Hart & Assoc.
Orlando, FL

Fabricator

Orlando Forge, Inc.
Winter Park, FL

This system includes more than 100 directional signs throughout the city. All were made of aluminum; some include real brass instruments. The hardware is stainless-steel painted with polyurethane paints.

Designers

Michael Horton, Larry Kennedy
Kramer + Kennedy Design
Honolulu, HI

Fabricator

EEC Industries Ltd.
North Vancouver, BC, Canada

The main entrance signs have individually cast brass letters with mirror-polished surfaces. They are 3/4 in. thick, mounted 3/4 in. from the wall surface to create a drop shadow. Room number signs (1235 in all) are of 3 1/2 x 5-in. Italian Perlato Sicilia marble with letters and numbers deep-etched and filled with brown paint to match the door color. The 18 outdoor pathway directionals, 35 health facility and four pool-area signs are aluminum with faux-finish paint. Tower identification signs consist of 6-in. Michelangelo-type letters sandblasted into Rojo Alacante marble. The "Registration," "Cashier" and "Concierge" signs have 16 x 2 x 4-in. Cocoa Dorata marble bases with half round edges to match the existing counters. The glass is 12 x 3/4 x 4 in. with 1/2-in. bevel, deep-etched sub-surface letters.

Designers
Sparky Potter
Wood & Wood Sign Co.
Waitsfield, VT
FORMA
Seattle, WA

Fabricator
Wood & Wood Sign Co.

A predominantly wooden sign system enhances the character of this wooden hotel built in 1891. Architectural elements from the hotel's porch were incorporated into the main signs; traditional "tip" details employed by island carpenters over the years were used in the traffic signs. Interior signs are combinations of wooden backgrounds and acrylic sign faces.

Designer
Steve Mysse
Sign and Design
Billings, MT

Fabricator
Sign and Design

The signage for Red Lodge Mountain Ski Resort ranges in size from 5 x 24 in. to 4 x 4 ft. Painted plywood was lettered with vinyl.

Designers

The Phoenix Zoo Design Dept.
Phoenix, AZ
Arizona State University Graphic Design Dept.
Phoenix, AZ

Fabricators

The Phoenix Zoo Design Dept.
The Studio
Tempe, AZ
GAR Industries, Inc. (metalwork)
Phoenix, AZ
Schmidt Metal Fabricators
Phoenix, AZ
Advance Metal Fabricator
Tempe, AZ

These signs are all of aluminum construction, utilizing special floating nuts and precision fabrication to ensure that components are interchangeable. Sizes range from 6 x 18 x 2 in. to 38 x 18 x 2 in. Color coatings are electrostatically applied polyester powder. Text and illustrations are screen-printed, with vinyl letters used for large type. All the panels received several finish coats of clear automotive urethane.

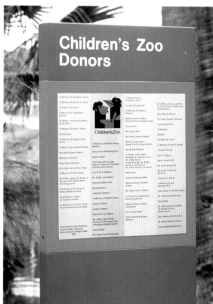

WALL-MOUNTED OR FACIA SIGNS

Even more than hanging or projecting signs, wall-mounted or facia signs are inherently subject to the confines of the buildings they identify. The category is defined, as the name implies, by their being "flush" mounted to the walls or facades of the respective buildings.

Designer
William Schoonmaker
Schoonmaker Architects
Durham, NH

Fabricator
Exeter Signworks
Exeter, NH

The owner of this architectural firm designed the "Big Pencil" as signage for his own office. The sign background is 3 x 4-ft., reinforced MDO with bulletin enamel and vinyl lettering. The pencil jprojects 2 ft. to the sharpened point and 4 ft. to the slightly worn eraser. The sign was fabricated from high-density foam epoxy, glued and cut to shape, and finished with auto enamel.

Designer
Bill Hanapple
Ad-Art, Inc.
Stockton, CA

Fabricator
Ad-Art, Inc.

An existing trademark was adapted to the arched entrance of this Emeryville, California center. The 2-ft. illuminated letters have red plastic faces and are pegged away from the background to provide white "halo" illumination, through translucent backs, around the red copy. Neon, in rainbow colors, follows the curvature of the arch and carries through the extensive use of neon elsewhere in the center.

Designer
Steve Mahler
S & S Sign Company
Seattle, WA

Fabricator
S & S Sign Company

The 20 1/2 x 8 1/2-ft. letters for the Boeing Employees Credit Union were mounted to a parapet wall on the 7th floor of the building. The halo-lit "B,C,U" letters were fabricated from welded aluminum. The faces were painted white and the side walls dark bronze. The "E" in the logo is a channel letter also fabricated from welded aluminum. Its face is pigmented fuchsia plastic. The sign is lit by 60ma double and triple tube 6500 white and rose neon.

Designer
Brian Kurzius
Adirondack Sign & Design
Saranac Lake, NY

Fabricator
Adirondack Sign & Design

This 21 x 48-in. sign combines cut-out pieces of wood composite, glass smalts and 23K gold with hand carving. The entire border, oval logo and ornaments were cut-out and then applied.

Designer
Ron Miriello
Miriello Grafico
San Diego, CA

Fabricator
Ultraneon Sign Co.
San Diego, CA

Made for an Italian restaurant, this multi-layered sign (10 x 10 ft.) comprises routed aluminum sheets. The continuous welds for both the facia and all sides have a seamless finish. An intricate design-and-fabrication system was used to prevent the different halo lights from interfering with each other and to keep the overall emphasis on the tomato. The main entrance and the top edge of the building front were trimmed with finished aluminum sheets coated with a layer of clear lacquer.

Designers

Hulme-Ridgeway Neon Sign Company
Anderson, SC
Options Design Group
Greenville, SC

Fabricator

Hulme-Ridgeway Neon Sign Company

This 8 x 8-ft. diagonal aluminum sign has routed aluminum squares with backlit acrylic mounted underneath. The copy is channel letters with acrylic faces mounted on top of the cabinet and internally-illuminated.

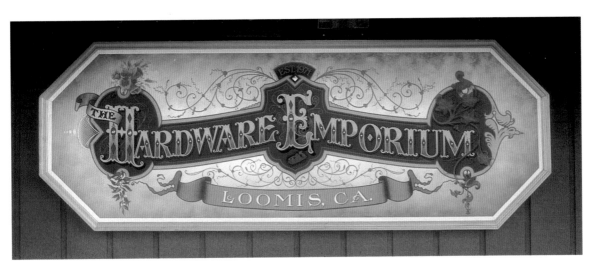

Designer

Jim Ingram
Jim Ingram Signs
Penryn, CA

Fabricator

Jim Ingram Signs

This 4 x 11-ft. sign has a brush-blended background, gilded upholstery tacks as letter decorations, an old block plane illustrated at the center, and a painted frame and matte.

Designer
Ad-Art, Inc.
Stockton, CA

Fabricator
Ad-Art, Inc.

This three-sided projecting sign canopy is fabricated of metal with a satin matte finish. The
sign units are inset flush with flat cut-out black
graphics on a white plastic background. The sign
is interior illuminated.

Designer
Jim Schultz
Smith, Nelson & Oatis
Denver, CO

Fabricator
Smith, Nelson & Oatis

This 3 x 10-ft. sign for a bus company was flat
painted on 1/2-in. MDO plywood.

Designer
John Cox
Thorough-Graphic
SignsLexington, KY

Fabricator
Thorough-Graphic Signs

This art gallery sign was cut to shape approximately 3 x 8 ft. from MDO. It features hand-painted lettering, borders and graphics.

Designer
Walt Disney Imagineering
Glendale, CA

Fabricator
Walt Disney Imagineering

This 2 x 15-ft. sign comprises neon exposed illumination, reverse pan channel letters and an expanded metal background.

Designer
Mark Oatis
Smith, Nelson & Oatis
Denver, CO

Fabricator
Smith, Nelson & Oatis

For Racines Restaurant, 75 ft. of frontage had to be created. The pan-channel steel cabinet at the front entry was adorned with colored aluminum raised elements (and colored neon behind). All scenes as well as the door were designed by the project team.

Designer
Vinick Associates
Hartford, CT

Fabricator
ARTeffects, Inc.
Hartford, CT

The primary storefront sign features 4 x 12-in. letters fabricated entirely of 3/16-in. white acrylic on metal pans. The letter faces have 11-color transition striping (magenta to process blue), screen-printed clear vinyl, applied. The sign is lit with 12 white argon tubing.

Designer
Reed Design Associates
Madison, WI

Fabricator
Reed Design Associates

This sign comprises polished bronze, etched and in-filled with red and black paint. It was designed for an old firehouse that was renovated and converted to office space in Madison, Wisconsin.

Designers
Elizabeth An and Jim Rizzo
San Francisco, CA
Tiempo Interiors
San Francisco, CA
Gianola & Sons, Inc.
Sausalito, CA

Fabricator
Jim Rizzo
Neon Works
San Francisco, CA

The Crustacean Restaurant specializes in roasted crab, and this original design was created to convey the restaurant's cuisine. The wave is 135 ft. long x 6 ft. tall, extending the full length of the building's facade; the wave is supported at the peaks by 1-in. conduit bent to the shape of the wave and extends 3 ft. above the building. The crab itself measures 5 x 6 ft. in 15mm fuchsia, and is mounted to the face of a polished aluminum can. The awning is outlined in 12mm deep aqua, and the polished stainless-steel face was cut-out so that the crab and the restaurant logo could be backlit through white acrylic.

Designer
David & Company
San Diego, CA

Fabricator
Ultraneon Sign Company
San Diego, CA

This internally-illuminated sheetmetal cabinet is laminated with brass-finish aluminum. The sign face is curved with routed copy. Finish detail and construction were essential in giving this sign the feel of being an extension of the building overhang structure.

Designer
Mark Oatis
Mark Oatis Designs
Denver, CO

Fabricator
Mark Oatis Designs

This 5 x 8-ft. sandblasted redwood sign was finished in stains and enamels.

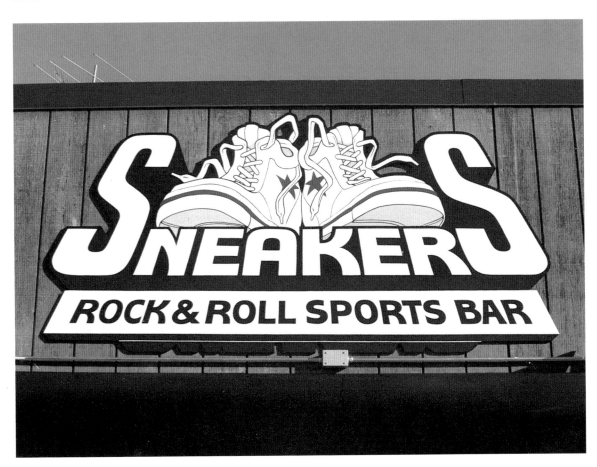

Designer
Mark Baty
Baty Art & Sign, Inc.
Waukee, IA

Fabricator
Baty Art & Sign, Inc.

This sign for a sports bar measures 4 x 8 ft.
Fabricated of MDO, it is enamel coated.

Designer
Gary Anderson
Bloomington Design
Bloomington, IN

Fabricator
Bloomington Design

This sign was flat painted in enamels on MDO.
The lettering, "The Daily Grind," is vinyl; "Sub
Shop" was cut-out of MDO, rounded and then
painted with enamels.

Designer
Gary Anderson
Bloomington Design
Bloomington, IN

Fabricator
Bloomington Design

This 3 x 7-ft. sign was sandblasted and carved from redwood with gilded pine letters. It has a latex finish.

Designers
Vital Signs
Pensacola, FL
PETERHANSREA
Birmingham, MI

Fabricator
Vital Signs

Measuring approximately 6 x 3 ft., this composite-wood sign utilizes a combination of high-density urethane and fiberglass for the bird heads, which are gilded.

Designer
Danny Febles
Strictly Neon
Boulder, CO

Fabricator
Strictly Neon

Neon colors of clear blue, veep green, purple, clear red, rose, clear gold, 6500 white, 4500 white, magenta, orange and turquoise were used in this signage for Stereo Image. The store entrance sign measures 8 x 3 ft.

Designer
Ray Guzman
Hoboken Sign Shop
Hoboken, NJ

Fabricator
Hoboken Sign Shop

The 20-ft. x 20-in. sign for a bar/saloon features 23K spun goldleaf. The 3D effect on the "D," "H" and "F" was achieved by airbrushing brown paint on top of the wet varnish over the 23K gold. The green gemstone was hand-painted with the burgundy rose panels indented in each letter. The banner was sponged in pastel blues, and outlined in pastel peach, all of which was painted over vinyl-cut letters. These were highlighted with airbrushing and outlined in rose. The floating shadow effect was also airbrushed. The sign's background was sponged in three deep purple enamels. The flowers were hand-painted in enamels. The decorative pinstriping motif was rendered in three colors.

Designer
Bill Hueg
Signs of Distinction
St. Paul, MN

Fabricator
Signs of Distinction

This 21 x 48-in. MDO sign has a dark green enamel background with ivory letters. The camera was done in lettering enamels.

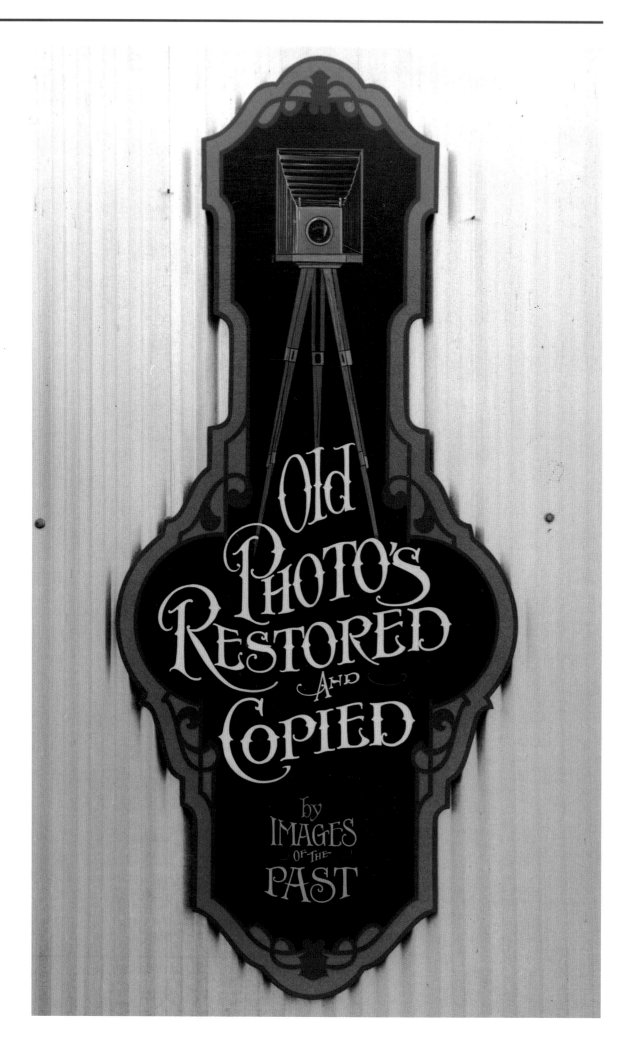

Designer
Krommenhoek, McKeown & Associates
San Diego, CA

Fabricator
Signtech Electrical Advertising, Inc.
San Diego, CA

The various signs for this cinema feature open
pan channel letters; routed aluminum faces with
pushed-through 1-in.-thick, frosted-edged, clear
acrylic; and first surface vinyl copy.

Designer
McMillan and Strauss Design
Welland, ON, Canada

Fabricator
Rustic Designs
Welland, On, Canada

Constructed of kiln-dried pine, this sign was sandblasted. Cut-outs and special moldings were used
for the lettering and flourishes.

Designer
Robertson Pick Creative Services
Vancouver, BC, Canada

Fabricator
John Peachey & Associates
N. Vancouver, BC, Canada

Pin-mounted on a rough rock wall, this 7 1/2 x 2 1/2-ft. sign features 23K gilded letters and long stem rose, fabricated from high-density foam. The backer has bevelled edges and a routed border and was finished with "verde gris" antique.

Designer
Kas Taylor
Castle Rock, CO

Fabricator
Kas Taylor

This 34 x 46-in. ellipse for a retail jewelry store was hand-carved from basswood. No routers or sandblasting was used. The sign was gilded with 23K gold.

Designer
Mark Oatis
Smith, Nelson & Oatis
Denver, CO

Fabricator
Smith, Nelson & Oatis

A nondescript white stucco building needed a facelift, so the designer used house paint on the stucco with various raised elements to provide the improvement. The signage measures approximately 35 x 14 ft.

Designer
Harri A. Aulto
Dimensional Stone Signs
Fairfield, IA

Fabricator
Dimensional Stone Signs

This 24 x 24-in. sign has a Mountain Rainbow natural marble plaque background with the logo cut from Olympus marble.

Designer
Ray Guzman
Hoboken Sign Shop
Hoboken, NJ

Fabricator
Hoboken Sign Shop

This 8 ft. x 30-in. sign for a vendor of fruit drinks, shakes and ice cream was hand-painted and air-brushed in enamels.

Designer
Fedele Musso
Ultra Neon
Jupiter, FL

Fabricator
Ultra Neon

Here, the client wanted an attention-getting display to enliven the grounds of his landscaping business. The 6 x 10-ft. display was mounted directly onto the stucco side of the client's building. Colors used: neon-blue pumped argon and neon; noviol gold pumped argon. The background was painted to match colors when lit.

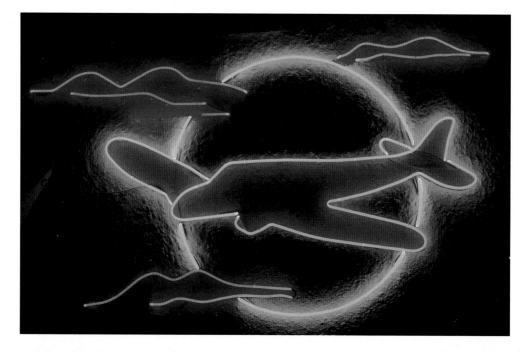

Designer
Franca B. Panetta
Enseicom Signs Inc.
Mount Royal, PQ, Canada

Fabricator
Enseicom Signs Inc.

This 16 x 16-ft. projecting backlit awning was designed to meet three criteria: to replace an old sign with one that reflected the new size and image of this fur coat retailer; to cover as much of the rundown facade of this building as city bylaws would permit; and to provide a sign that had a homogenous appearance while at the same time functioning as a multi-tenant sign.

Designers
Karen Beane, Jason Beane
Rapid Sign of FL, Inc.
Ft. Meyers, FL

Fabricator
Rapid Sign of FL, Inc.

This 10 x 12-ft. sign, gracing a restaurant located on the Gulf of Mexico, reflects a casual, beach lifestyle. The sign face was painted and air-brushed for the effect of sky, water and beach. Graphics were rendered with "high-performance" vinyl with a clear polyurethane finish. A variety of neon colors outlines the main features of artwork; the name of the restaurant was produced in open-face channel letters. A clear acrylic face was installed for safety purposes.

Designer
Gary Anderson
Bloomington Design
Bloomington, IN

Fabricator
Bloomington Design

This 3 x 12-ft. MDO sign was painted with enamels. The background was airbrushed to simulate grass.

Designers
Bill Cawthon
Signtech Electrical Adv., Inc.
Lemon Grove, CA
Brooks Graham
Graham Design
New Orleans, LA
Nick Poulos, James M. Williams
Landmark Theater Corp.
Los Angeles, CA

Fabricator
Signtech Electrical Adv., Inc.

For Hillcrest Cinemas, the geometric shapes were constructed of aluminum, painted in various colors and then outlined with various colors of single-tube neon. The copy comprises 5-in.-deep, open, pan-channel letters with 11-watt yellow bulbs outlined with single-tube tangerine yellow. Message centers to the left and right of the logo also were included, as was the architectural element with its square-tubed structure and wire-mesh screen (which helps to fill the void area of the building and support the sign).

Designer
Universal Studios
Orlando, FL

Fabricator
Wood & Wood Signs
Waitsfield, CT

Fabricated with a composite board background, this 12 x 2 1/2-ft. sign features composite board letters, trim boards and sailing ships painted on slabs of pine. The ships were painted with acrylic artist's paints and varnished over; the rest of the sign was finished with exterior house paints.

Designers
Mark Oatis, Jim Schultz
Smith, Nelson & Oatis
Denver, CO
RTKL Associates, Inc.
Baltimore, MD

Fabricator
Smith, Nelson & Oatis

Depicting different types of fare offered in a shopping mall food court, these five figures are each about 5 ft. tall. One is a metal "directional" figure, pointing the way to "Boulevard Cafes." The fully dimensional figures were built of a foam material.

Designer
John Cox
Thorough-Graphic Signs
Lexington, KY

Fabricator
Thorough-Graphic Signs

All effects are flat in this 4 x 8-ft sign for a real estate developer.

Designer
Mark Oatis
Smith, Nelson & Oatis
Denver, CO

Fabricators
Smith, Nelson & Oatis
Independent Sign Co. (metal work)
Denver, CO

For a gaming parlor in Cripple Creek, CO, this 5 x 6-ft. sign was constructed of pan-channel panels of 1/8-in aluminum. Automotive sign enamels were used for the finish, and this was overlaid with 23K gilt PVC. The flourishes and letters were carved.

Designer
Exhibit House, Ltd.
Elk Grove Village, IL

Fabricator
Vintage Sign Shoppe
Woodstock, IL

Measuring 30 x 48 in., this clear redwood sign has a sandblasted background.

Designer
Nancy Bennett
Dannco
Centerville, IA

Fabricator
Dannco

This 26 x 96-in. sign welcomes visitors to a restored 1912 hotel. Composed of MDO plywood with a brick-mold frame, the sign was hand-lettered and gilded. The cat and striping were done by hand with lettering enamels. The background is smalts.

Designer
Brother Zank
Custom Craftsman
Sevierville, TN

Fabricator
Custom Craftsman

The 4 x 6-ft. wall-mounted sign for this upscale southern dinner theater has a cedar beveled and marbleized frame, rabbeted to the face. The horizontal wrap is graze-blasted cedar, knotched to drop back against the face. "Nashville South" is 1/2-in sawn composite board with an airbrushed fade.

Designer
Ray Guzman
Hoboken Sign Shop
Hoboken, NJ

Fabricator
Hoboken Sign Shop

For the main panel of this sign for a bar, the background was sponged in three colors (marbled). Letters were airbrushed, banners sponged and rules gilded. For the center piece, the oval was sandblasted and routed, then trimmed with goldleaf. The portrait was hand-painted with artist's oil colors.

Designer
Graphic Solutions
San Diego, CA

Fabricator
Signtech Electrical Adv., Inc.
Lemon Grove, CA

This sign utilizes reverse pan, halo-lit letters as well as open pan letters with double-tube exposed neon. The neon waves were fabricated from exposed-border neon; the fish were made from aluminum (with etched scales).

Designer
Media Concepts Corp.
Boston, MA

Fabricator
Paul McCarthy's Carving Place
Scituate, MA

This gallery sign was hand-carved on 2-in. eastern pine.

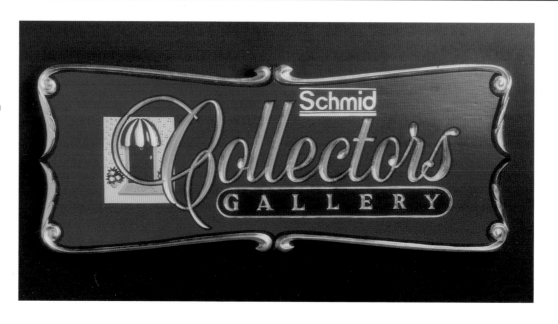

Designer
Brad Johnson
Brad Johnson Signs
Corvallis, OR

Fabricator
Brad Johnson Signs

The beveled edges of this 5 1/2 x 2-ft. sign were sponged to create an electric feel. Convex letters for "Bagel" have four shades and the bagels themselves have seven. A common "light source" at the top and right adds depth.

Designer
Commercial Signs
Mt. Clemens, MI

Fabricator
Commercial Signs

The chrome, red-acrylic-faced channel letters for this video store sign are mounted on a flat-black, aluminum raceway that incorporates a mirrored, neon-lit "infinity" panel, reminiscent of an old movie marquee. The sign is further enhanced by blue neon halo lighting. Overall size is 4 x 17 ft.

Designers
Cecil Burns, Jim deRoin
Boyd Design Group
Englewood, CO

Fabricators
Boyd Design Group
John Hoover
Englewood, CO

This 3 ft. 4-in. x 11 ft. x 1 ft. 4-in. sign was created for a business in historic Breckenridge, CO. The wood-composite background features multiple layers of sandblasting. The pictorial elements were hand-carved and hand-painted in acrylics. The dimensional letters were copper-gilded and applied to the airbrushed, purple outline.

Designer
Walt Disney World Design & Engineering
Lake Buena Vista, FL

Fabricators
Walt Disney World Mill Shop
Walt Disney World Paint Shop

This is the entry ID sign (28 x 50 in.) for the head office of Walt Disney World. The main body of the sign is sandblasted grain cedar and utilizes a black smalts background. The ribbon was airbrushed with lettering enamel. "Central Shops" comprises dimensional letters, cut from 23K gilded chipboard, then rounded off and attached with slow-set epoxy. The border was copper-leafed and hand-brushed. All graphics and lettering were done with enamel paint.

Designer
Albert Quimby
Bert Graphix
Pompton Lakes, NJ

Fabricator
Bert Graphix

This design, airbrushed on MDO and foam board, was executed to match the company truck. The lettering fades from fire red to orange to primrose yellow.

Designer
Rob Kauth
Spaz Graphix
Franklin, WI

Fabricator
Spaz Graphix

This sign was constructed of 1/2-in. MDO and measures 8 x 16 ft. The background was painted to resemble tongue-and-groove boarding. The center panel was marbleized and airbrushed to add dimension. "Mountain Corner Store" was glazed on and then outlined, to appear carved.

Designer
Jeffrey Dean
Sign Design Studios
Sarasota, FL

Fabricator
Sign Design Studios

This sign for a muscle building competition is fabricated of cut-out MDO, airbrushed and suspended in front of a black drape. Measurements: 4 x 8 ft.

Designer
John Cox
Thorough-Graphic Signs
Lexington, KY

Fabricator
Thorough-Graphic Signs

This 20 x 96-in. MDO plywood sign was hand-painted, distressed, gilded and antiqued to replicate turn-of-the-century stationery. The sign also features molding.

Designer
Paul McCarthy
Paul McCarthy's Carving Place
Scituate, MA

Fabricator
Paul McCarthy's Carving Place

This sign was hand-carved from 2-in.-thick eastern pine. It measures 2 x 4 ft.

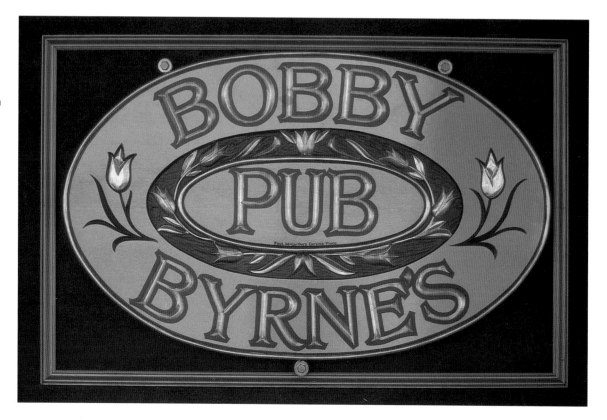

Designer
Randy Glen
Pacific Neon Co.
Delta, BC, Canada

Fabricator
Pacific Neon Co.

The lettering was hand-painted on gray slatwall for this sign. The letters are also outlined in the same color neon. The soccer ball is a "blow-molded" half sphere, sprayed with acrylic and backlit with neon.

SPECIALTY SIGNS

Three specialized types of signs are grouped together in this final section, including window lettering, glass signs, and wall murals and graphics. Whereas window lettering and glass signs have a commonality of application surface and share materials and techniques used in decoration, wall murals and graphics might stand alone as a category due to its own special characteristics. Window lettering and glass signs are predominately decorated on the reverse side so that the lettering and/or graphics show through the surface; walls, which may be either interior or exterior, are more typical of other sign types in that the copy and/or graphics are surface applied.

Designer
Douglas Evers
General Sign
Bloomington, IN

Fabricator
General Sign

The logo measures 16 in. on this window sign. It was lettered in 23K gold with a black outline.

Designer
William Cochran
The Signworks
Walkersville, MD

Fabricator
The Signworks

This sign is one of twin 4-ft. window signs that were hand-painted with airbrushed details on the pictorial. The lettering is dove gray with a forest green outline and shadow. The circle is teal blue with letters outlined in dark blue. The background is painted bronze and gold.

Designer
Swartzendruber Signs
Anamosa, IA

Fabricator
Swartzendruber Signs

The design was rendered in reverse on the inside of the window in lettering enamels. "Wagonload Antiques" measures approximately 3 x 4 ft., while the four top panels range from 10 x 34 in. to 10 x 60 in.

Designer
Liza Netzley
Signs by Liza
Naperville, IL

Fabricator
Signs by Liza

The sign is approximately 2 x 7 ft. "Toenniges" has deep Damar texture. All copy is 23K gold with burnished outlines. The scroll is 23K gold with an asphaltum wash. The diamond is 18K matte and burnished gold. The outlines are enamel paint.

Designer
Noel Weber
Classic Sign Studio
Boise, ID

Fabricator
Classic Sign Studio

This sign features a combination of goldleaf, varnish textures and color blends.

Designer
Henri Mooy
Dutchboy Signs
St. Peters, MO

Fabricator
Dutchboy Signs

These two windows are each 5 ft. high x 6 ft. wide. Lettering enamels were used to produce stippled, graduated colors. The outlines were bronzed, and the ovals feature red abalone shell. The bass was rendered in lettering enamel on the inside of the window.

Designer
Smith, Nelson & Oatis
Denver, CO

Fabricator
Smith, Nelson & Oatis

Spanning 18 x 48 in., this sign was executed using 23K goldleaf, enamels and airbrushing.

Designers
Noel Weber, Kevin Mills, Todd Hanson
Classic Sign Studio
Boise, ID

Fabricator
Classic Sign Studio

These signs are on the display wall of Classic Sign Studio. The overall display is 10 x 12 ft.

Designer
Randy Workman
Heartwood Signs
Gulfport, MS

Fabricator
Heartwood Signs

This 2 x 4-ft. glass panel has a glue-chipped background, 23K gold outlines, blended centers and a split-shade marbled panel. "And" was acid etched; the medallions are 18K copperleaf scrolls. "Attorneys at Law" was glue-chipped and gilded with 23K gold.

Designer
Ray Guzman
Hoboken Sign Shop
Hoboken, NJ

Fabricator
Hoboken Sign Shop

On this window of a sports bar and restaurant, enamels were utilized for the two athletes. The lettering was gilded with 23K gold and silverleaf, then outlined in artist's transparent oil colors.

Designers
Ray Guzman
Joe Spano (logo)
Hoboken Sign Shop
Hoboken, NJ

Fabricator
Hoboken Sign Shop

Here, two-tone "polygold" vinyl with a black outline was used to achieve a hand-cut, etched look.

Designer
Nick Clemens
Dayton, OH

Fabricator
John Chrisman, Signwriter
Kettering, OH

This sign has a 3 x 4-ft. x 1/2-in.-thick glass panel, which is gilded. It's double-faced on a single piece of glass, and hand-rendered with brushes in 12 colors without any computer assistance.

Designer
Chris Brabander
Brecksville, OH

Fabricator
Argus Images
Lexington, OH

This 18 x 9-in. sign was created with frosted vinyl. The shop is located within a nature center whose primary function is education about natural resources and conservation.

Designer
Robby Rucker
Festival Sign Service
Gainesville, FL

Fabricator
Festival Sign Service

The 79 x 36-in. door was made from sand-blasted redwood, and gilded with 23K and 18K goldleaf, white gold and copperleaf. It was painted with lettering enamels, and some areas were airbrushed. The oval glass window is 16 x 20 in. The window was glue-chipped and gilded with 23K, 18K and white gold. The burnished letters have matte 18K centers, and mother-of-pearl ovals are in each central letter. The wings were created with blended enamels.

Designer
Carol J. Chapel
Watermark
Philomath, OR

Fabricator
Watermark

This 18 x 24-in. window sign is burnished and matte 23K goldleaf, bronze powder and paint. The backing was screen-printed.

Designer
William Cochran
The Signworks
Walkersville, MD

Fabricator
The Signworks

The sign shown is one of twin 46-in. window signs that are screen-printed, hand-painted and gilded. The illustration of a well known raconteur was hand-drawn and then screen-printed on the glass. "R.J. Jilly's" was gilded; the subcopy was outlined in black and apricot; the pictorial is black and cream, outlined in cream and apricot; and the lines and flourishes are gilded.

Designer
Brad Johnson
Brad Johnson Signs
Corvallis, OR

Fabricator
Brad Johnson Signs

A 4 x 10-ft. MDO plywood panel provides the background for this bakery and cafe signage. "Kinetic" letters were cut out and airbrushed, and the background was set off with spacers. The cut-out letters for "bagel" were done in two-tone convex. An airbrush was used to spatter the cut-out panels with bagels.

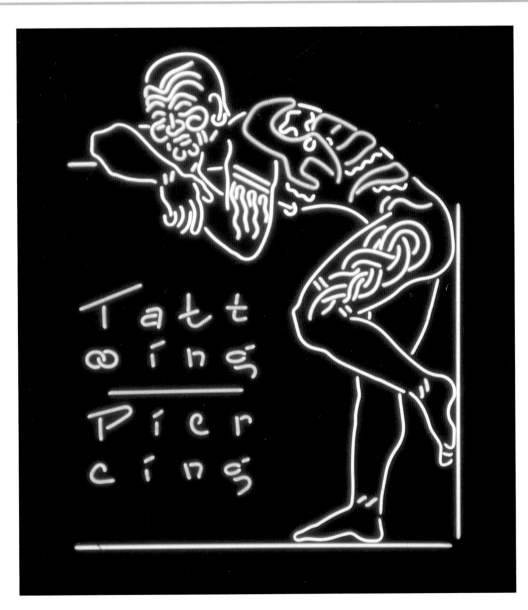

Designer
Patrick D. Meyer
San Francisco, CA

Fabricators
Patrick D. Meyer
Robert Jansen
Concord, CA

For a studio specializing in "modern-primitive" tattooing and piercing, this original design was created. It consists of 120 ft. of 10mm neon tubing mounted on 4 x 6 ft. smoked acrylic backing.

Designer
Bill Hueg
Signs of Distinction
St. Paul, MN

Fabricator
Signs of Distinction

This 15 x 29-in. sign has a 23K burnished gold outline with lime green inline and 18K Damar varnish centers. The dingbats are 23K burnished gold, green and copper bronze powder. The split shades and shamrock are transparent glazes, backed with lettering enamel. The "Q" has abalone shell and plaid burnish in glazed 16K goldleaf.

Designers
Ben McKnight
Sharper Images
Bayfield, WI
Kathi Dunn (logo)

Fabricator
Sharper Images

This 49 x 35-in. sign has a glue-chipped border with a frosted design. The upper copy is gilded with 23K gold. The cherry wood frame is connected to a 3-in. oak extension jamb. The back is covered with black fabric.

Designer
Temptations!
Corvallis, OR

Fabricator
Carol Chapel
Watermark
Corvallis, OR

This 40 x 65-in. sign utilizes 23K and 12K goldleaf, aluminum leaf, bronze powder, enamel, artist's oils and prisma glitter.

Designer
Chris Shuster
Son Signs
Inglis, FL

Fabricator
Son Signs

Approximately 5 x 7 ft., this sign was reverse-painted and airbrushed. The gold pinstriping was done with micas and backed up with similar colors. The knife blade features aluminum leaf. The oval has a stippled background. The shadows and highlights on the split shade were lightly rubbed with steel wool to increase "action." Otherwise, lettering enamels were used.

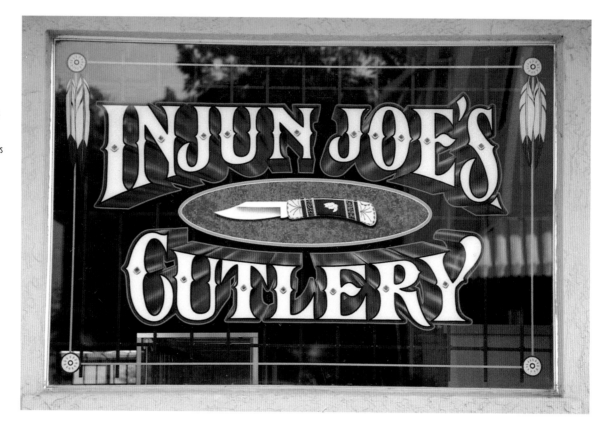

Designer
Mike Sheehan
Classic Sign & Mirror, Inc.
Pensacola, FL

Fabricator
Classic Sign & Mirror, Inc.

Shown is one of four shaded and etched safety glass panels that range in size from 3 ft. 6 in. square to 3 ft. 6 in. x 5 ft., all framed in oak.

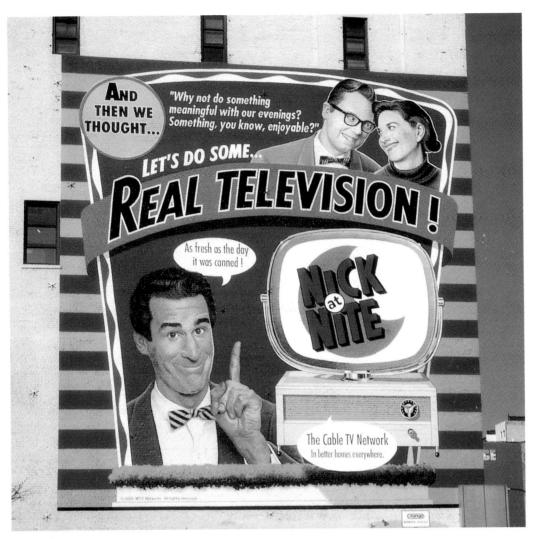

Designer
Jerry Johnson
Orange Outdoor Adv., Inc.
Brooklyn, NY

Fabricator
Orange Outdoor Adv., Inc.

For MTV Networks' "Nick at Nite"—a vintage re-run television/cable network, this 48 x 46-ft. painted wall sign in lower Manhattan targets 18- to 35-year-olds who might be tired of major network programming.

Designers
Mark Oatis, Jim Schultz
Smith, Nelson & Oatis
Denver, CO

Fabricator
Smith, Nelson & Oatis

For this micro brewery and restaurant, the 40 x 60-ft. sign was designed to simulate a faded antique wall sign. It was executed in lettering enamels on primed brick, then glazed with varnish to "distress" the entire job.

Designer
Joshua Winer
Architectural Murals
Arlington, MA

Fabricators
Architectural Murals
Ackerley Communications
Stoneham, MA

This 50 x 50-ft. trompe-l'oeil mural was created using bulletin enamels on a stucco brick wall.

Designer
Mark Oatis
Smith, Nelson & Oatis
Denver, CO

Fabricator
Smith, Nelson & Oatis

This 19 x 31-ft. mural was painted on brick with lettering enamels. The design was adapted from an actual brand of cigars sold in the early 1900s. The copy and pictorial are original designs.

Designers
Paul Wilson
Middletown, MD
William Cochran
The Signworks
Walkersville, MD
Bill Hueg
St. Paul, MN

Fabricators
The Signworks
Bill Hueg

This 8 1/2 x 90-ft. mural was created for an upscale shopping mall. Hand-painted on-site in acrylics, the landscape is visible from the interior of the restaurant and from the cafe seating area.

Designers
Mark Oatis
Smith, Nelson & Oatis
Denver, CO
Bill Hueg
St. Paul, MN

Fabricator
Smith, Nelson & Oatis

This 18 x 42-in. mural was rendered in oils over rough stone.

Designer
William Cochran
The Signworks
Walkersville, MD

Fabricators
The Signworks
Mark Oatis, Carolyn Parker, Colleen Clapp, Ed Barker, Bettina Messersmith
Denver, CO

This two-story trompe l'oeil mural entitled "Egress" was hand-painted on a blank stucco wall. It includes a three-color fade in the sky (purple/blue/green); airbrushed clouds; fades and glazes in illusory woodworks to heighten reality.

Designer
Brechin Morgan
Morgan Sign Co.
Norwalk, CT

Fabricator
Morgan Sign Co.

These 8 x 16-ft. wall murals were created with acrylic paint on a white brick wall. Gray shadows were added to make them "pop" off the wall. The overall size is 32 x 76 ft. Three people spent three weeks to complete the project.

Designers
Mark Oatis, Todd Hoffman, Sharon Feder
Smith, Nelson & Oatis
Denver, CO

Fabricator
Smith, Nelson & Oatis

This 16 x 24-ft. mural depicts a scene along the "Gilpin Tramway" route. The substrate is steel, and the "posterized" billboard-style pictorial was created with enamels.

Designers
Mark Oatis, Jim Schultz
Smith, Nelson & Oatis
Denver, CO

Fabricator
Smith, Nelson & Oatis

This 26 x 32-ft. mural depicts a fictional coffee. The design was created with lettering enamels on brick, and then it was distressed to suggest antiquity.

Designers
William Cochran, Colleen Clapp
The Signworks
Walkersville, MD

Fabricators
Keith Weaver, Phil Snyder
The Signworks
Baltimore, MD

This 10 1/2 x 38-ft. trompe l'oeil landscape mural was hand-painted in acrylics on the back wall of an architectural niche in a mall's food court. The chef figure seated on the rail duplicates the chef logo found throughout the mall complex. Even the mural's painted columns were rendered to match others in the mall.

Designer
Daniel Dillon
Dillon Design Associates
Cohoes, NY

Fabricator
Aerial Luft Company
Castleton, NY

The hot air balloon with passenger design was painted in enamels on a 125-ft.-high water tower that is 25 ft. in diameter.

Designer
MW Reklameprodukties
Boven-Leeuwen, Netherlands

Fabricator
MW Reklameprodukties

For this 10 x 16-ft. furniture-firm signage, the designer used a frosted vinyl film. The lettering changes color according to the weather.

Designers
William Cochran
The Signworks
Walkersville, MD
Mark Oatis, Keith Knecht
Denver, CO

Fabricators
The Signworks
Mark Oatis, Carolyn Parker, Bettina Messersmith
Denver, CO

This 11 x 30-ft. historically accurate Prohibition-era advertising mural was entirely brush-painted in four days. Forty colors and the following were used: posterized pictorial; convex script with royal purple and amber shades; a marbleized sign panel with a convexed border; striped and faded letters on "Capper;" highlights and jazz shadows on the panel copy; trompe l'oeil columns and "woodwork," including beam "supporting" roof; four-color stippled and faded background; and a three-color fade in "Bottle Capper" and "The," which are double-outlined.

Designer
Per Jacobson
The Design Works
Vancouver, BC, Canada

Fabricators
Kate Clifford Signs
W. Vancover, BC, Canada
Up-Sign (installation)
Vancouver, BC, Canada

For The City in the Park — a building development — 3/4-in.-thick MDO was used, and the headers were made of hand-cut vinyl. The screened building illustration on the right was executed with computer-cut vinyl. The center panel had to be curved for the mounted photo.

Designer
Hornsey Advertising
Dallas, TX

Fabricator
Wood Signs
Dallas, TX

This 8 x 16-ft. sign was made of 3/4-in. painted MDO panels. The rendering is a separate piece.

Designers
Sparky Potter
Wood and Wood Signs
Waitsfield, VT
T.J. Boyle, Architects
Burlington, VT
Coventry Development L.P.
Linthicum, MD

Fabricator
Wood and Wood Signs

The background of this 5 x 7 1/2-ft. sign is laminated MDO, with the prismatic molding painted in two colors. The upper slab is a pine lamination with carved and gilded letters. The lower slab is MDO with gold vinyl copy. The posts are rough hemlock.

Designers
David Hornblow, Karie McKinley
The Design Works
Vancouver, BC, Canada

Fabricator
Clay Signs
Vancouver, BC, Canada

For this signage at Nordel Business Park, plywood and paint were used. The signage "grew" in size during the construction, in five different phases, to a height of 40 ft. at completion.

Designers
Charles R. Lohre, Christina Corey
Lohre & Associates, Inc.
Cincinnati, OH

Fabricator
Lohre & Associates, Inc.

This 10th anniversary display for annual neighborhood festival includes four 2 x 2-ft. columns of expanded plastic material. The graphics are painted with lettering enamels and some vinyl lettering. Attached are digital scans and custom color prints of prior event posters. The display can be collapsed for transportation.

Designer
Daniel Dillon
Dillon Design Associates
Cohoes, NY

Fabricator
Dillon Design Associates

This 6-ft. high x 3-ft. wide sign was made with a wood-composite panel, and the oval is a 3/4-in.-thick piece of the same material. This raised panel has a marbleized background with 23K spun goldleaf lettering, a gilded finial and custom-fabricated colonial crown caps made of poplar. The remaining copy is a combination of hand lettering and vinyl. The pressure-treated post was decorated with more wood-composite, raised panels. The custom millwork on the sign was designed to complement the traditional interior and exterior trim work on the home.

Designers
Per Jacobsen, David Hornblow
The Design Works
Vancouver, BC, Canada

Fabricators
Clay Signs
Vancouver, BC, Canada

At Cathedral Place in Vancouver, the client had demolished the building previously occupying the site; the new barricade was designed to generate both goodwill and public interest. For this construction barricade, measuring 20 ft. x one city block (the ruler alone measured 27 ft.), spruce, steel, foam and plywood were used.

Designers
Les Roe, Renee Immel
The Phoenix Zoo Design Dept.
Phoenix, AZ

Fabricators
The Phoenix Zoo Design Dept.
Phoenix Tent and Awning
Phoenix, AZ

This display was constructed of 2 x 4s, 31 x 31-in. yellow banners and a 59 x 59-in. blue banner. Besides individual site signs, it includes a money collection box and promotional information for a new feature.

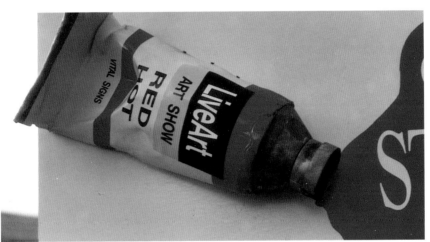

Designer
Chip Spirson
Vital Signs
Pensacola, FL

Fabricator
Vital Signs

Pictured is one of two 4 x 8-ft. MDO signs. The paint tube was constructed from styrene bent with a torch; the neck of the tube is turned wood. The sign company did not install the signs, which will be re-used for successive shows.

Designer
Daniel Dillon
Dillon Design Associates
seriesCohoes, NY

Fabricator
Dillon Design Associates

This single-face, 8 x 4-ft. flat painted sign was rendered on 1/2-in. MDO. The raised, cut-out logo is a simulated, brushed-brass laminate. The custom-fabricated fence ornamentation complements the arch of the traditional estate homes being built there.

INDEX

DESIGNERS

Adirondack Sign & Design 60, 103
ARTeffects, Inc. 38, 81, 86
Ad-Art, Inc. 106
Anderson, Gary 7, 37, 41, 42, 55, 63, 111, 112, 121
Andre Probst Creative Design, Inc. 6, 9
Arbough, Curtis 84
Ashton, David 50
Aulto, Harri A. 117

Bartlett, Denise 70
Baty, Mark 111
Beane, Karen 13, 120
Beane, Jason 120
Beck, Gregory 55
Becker, Rick 93
Beier, Terry 92
Bell, Gary 78
Bellina, Andy 58
Bennett, Nancy 74, 124
Bentsen, Paul 61
Bogdan, Robert 25
Bolin, Tom 90
Bollina, Andrew 14
Bonnette, Mark 59
Bouma, Scott 8
Brabander, Chris 138
Brewer, Don 45, 66
Bright and Associates (Bullwhackers) 94
Burns, Cecil 127

Cawthan, Bill 121
Chapel, Carol J. 140
Clapp, Colleen 150
Clemens, Nick 138
Cochran, William 76, 132, 140, 147, 148, 150, 152
Cody, Dale (Womack's) 94
Commercial Signs 127
Communication Arts 80
Cooke, Jay 26
Corey, Christina 155
Coventry Development L.P. 154
Cox, Jim 107, 123
Cox, John 123, 129
Cusick, Joe 43

Dail, Bob 93
Danieley, James B. II 27
David and Company 110
Dawley, Kai 41
DeRobbio, Bob 75
DeRoin, Jim 127
Dean, Jeffery 129

Degnen Associates, Inc. 92
Design Works, The 60
Desoto, Rufus 56
Dever, Thomas J. 80
Dillon, Daniel 26,58 ,67 151, 155, 157
Duda, Dave 72
Dunn, Kathi 143
Dunphy, Tracy 26

Eckman, Merv 28, 82, 83, 87
Envirographics, Inc. 83
Euers, Douglas 132
Exhibit House, Ltd. 124

Febles, Danny 113
Federspiel, Eric 13
Field, Anothy 65
Fox-Suarez Signs 52
Foxwoods Casino 86
Freeby, Dwayne E. 69
Full Moon Signs and Graphics 27

Garnity, Susannah and Stephen 40
Gianola & Sons, Inc. 109
Giposon, Larry 22
Glaser Associates, Inc. 44
Glen, Randy 130
Gompert, Fritz 21
Goodwyn, W.H. III 24
Gorsky, Nickie 49
Graham, Brooks 121
Graphic Solutions 126
Grate Signs, Inc. 28
Guzman, Ray 113, 118, 125, 137

Hanapple, Bill 102
Hannaman, Elton 48, 63, 71
Hanson, Todd 64, 71, 136
Harding, David M. 90
Harley, Jeff 93
Harrison, Lisa 97
Hedrick, Bob 68
Hendel, Dana 20
Hendrickson, Dick 85
Hoffman, Todd (Bull Durham) 94
Hoffman, Todd 149
Homsey Advertising 153
Hornblow, David 82, 88, 154, 156
Horton, Michael 98
Hubbard, Ann 68
Hueg, Bill 94 (Bull Durham, Womack's), 114,142, 144, 147
Hulme-Ridgeway Neon Sign Co. 105
Hutchinson, Lisa 31

Immel, Renee 156
Ingram, Jim 105
Ireland and Peachey 88
Ireland, Ross 48, 73
Ivey, Bennett, Harris and Walls 84

Jacobsen, Per 88, 153, 156
Janssen, Bruce (sign design) 86
Johnson, Brad 127, 141
Johnson, Jerry 145

Kauth, Rob 129
Kennedy, Larry 98
King, Brian (Turf Club) 94
Kinnunen, Michael 34, 87
Kinnunen, Michael 87
Knecht, Keith 152
Kramer, Eric 39
Krause, Bob 59
Krommenhoek, McKeown and Associates 115
Kuipers, Steve 46
Kurzius, Brian 60, 103

Lohre, Charles R. 155
Long, Richard 94
Lorel Marketing Group 36
Luthmann Brothers Woodcarving and Sign Co. 18, 22, 79, 85

MW Reklameprodukties 152
Mahler, Steve 103
Maine, David and Laura 62
Manning, Edward 64
Marynell, Tonia 10
McCarthy, Paul 15, 130
McGoldrick, Peter 11
McKinley, Karie 154
McKnight, Ben 44, 143
McMillan and Strauss Design 115
Media Concepts Corp. 126
Meyer, Patrick D. 141
Miller, Steven L. 74
Miller, Will 47, 59
Mills, Kevin 64, 71, 136
Miriello, Ron 104
Mooy, Henri 135
Moquin, Meredith 31
Morgan, Brechin 91, 149
Mozdzen, Joe 97
Musso, Fedele 118
Mysse, Steve 99

Najarian, Lynda 46
Nelson, Ann 54
Neon Products 53

Netzley, Liza 134
New England Design 86

O'Brien, Dan 49, 76
O'Donnell, Cheryl Long 94
Oatis, Mark 12, 40, 56, 97, 108, 110, 117, 122, 123, 145, 146, 147,149, 150, 152
Oatis, Mark (all except Bullwhackers and Bull Durham) 94
Openwood Studios Inc. 68
Osburn, Mike 79
Osonio, Angel 41

Panetta, Franca B. 119
Penfold, Neale 72
PETERHANSREA 78, 112
Phoenix Zoo Design Department, The 100
Pierson, Bill 72
Poanessa, Peter 15, 30, 51, 53
Potter, Sparky 36, 37, 43, 52, 61, 69, 96, 99, 154
Poulos, Nick 121
Putjenter, Joe 30

Quimby, Albert 128

Rauh, Good, Darlo and Barnes 34, 95
Reed Design Associates 109
Reithofer, Karen 65
Rhodes, Gary 34, 47
Rizzo, Elizabeth Ann and Jim 109
Robertson Pick Creative Services 116
Roe, Les 156
Roger Sherman Partners, Inc. 62
Rogers, Monte G. 21
Rosen, Lawrin 14
RTKL, Inc. 122
Rucker, Robby 139

Schoomaker, William 102
Schoos, Barb 66
Schultz, Jim (Wild Card) 94
Schultz, Jim 97, 106, 122, 145, 150
Shaughnessy Hart and Associates 98
Shaw, Bill 65
Sheehan, Mike 9, 10, 17, 144
Showalter, David 70
Schuster, Chris 113, 144
Siegrist, Ken 73
Sign Consultants, Inc. 18, 60
Sign Crafters, Inc. 8
Signage, Inc. 31, 65
Silva, Glenn 23
Sindaire, Steve 32
Smith, Larry Garcia 56

Smith, Nelson and Oatis 136
Soloman, Ivan 68
Spano, Joe 137
Sparks, Udita 49
Spirson, Chip 37, 67, 157
Squires, Debbie 45
Stamper, Gary 19, 70
Stenberg, John 16, 29, 88
Stenko, John 12
Stephens, Inc. (logo) 86
Stiltner, Forest 84
Sutton, Stephen 65
Swartzenduber Signs 133

Taylor, Kas 116
Taylor, Mark 11, 85, 90
Temptations! 143
Tiempo Interiors 109
T. J. Boyle, Architect 154
Tri-Ad Advertising (Diamond Lil's) 94
True, Neil 46

Universal Studios 43, 122
Uxbridge Carvers 51

Van Dyke, John 95
Vinick and Associates 108
Vital Signs 112

Walt Disney Imageering 107
Walt Disney World Design and Engineering 128
Wanbaugh, Jon 7, 13, 20, 72
Weber, Noel 19, 43, 64, 71, 134, 136
Weingartner, Peter A. 16
Wells, Willie 35, 38, 46
Whiteway, Abadh 76
Wicks, Constance Hesse 94
Williams, Douglas 6, 35, 54
Williams, James M. 121
Williams, Marge 42
Williamson, Billy 75
Wilson, Paul 147
Winer, Joshua 146
Wisemen, Chris 68
Woodmark 23, 80
Workman, Randy 136
Wygonik, Mark 81

Yancey Sign Art, Inc. 25
Yaseen, Kraig 39
Yashinski, Julie 29

Zank, Brother 125

FABRICATORS

ADCON Signs 28, 82, 83, 87
AMG Sign Company 45, 66
ARTeffects, Inc. 14, 38, 81, 86, 108
Accent Signing Company 24
Ad-Art, Inc. 102, 106
Adirondack Sign and Design 60,
Advance Metal Fabricator 100
Aerial Luft Company 151
Andre Probst Creative Design Inc. 6, 9
Andy Bellina 58
Architectural Murds 146
Argus Images 138
Art and Design (installation) 41
Artistry Signs 30
Artsign Design 16, 29, 88

Back Bay Awning Co. 39
Bamtech Signs and Graphics 10
Baty Art and Sign, Inc. 111
Bentsen Signs 61
Bert Graphix 128
Bloomington Design 7, 37, 41, 42, 55,
   63, 111, 112, 121
Bob Krause Wood Graphics 59
Bulin Masonry 90
Boyd Design Group 127
Brad Johnson Signs 127, 141

Carlos Dania Contractors (installation) 41
Carol Chapel 143
Christy Signs 46
Classic Sign Studio 19, 43, 64, 71, 134,
   136
Classic Sign and Mirror, Inc. 9, 10, 17,
   144
Clay Signs 154, 156
Cleveland Metroparks Graphics 14
CoSigns 94
Coast Graphics and Signs, Inc. 73
Cold Spring Granite 18
Columbus Sign Co. 92
Commercial Signs 127
Curt Oxford Woodcarver, Inc. 81
Custom Craftsman 125
Cypress Carving, Ltd. 48

Dannco 74, 124
David Design 70
Dawley Carved Signs 41, 54
Design Systems 27
Dillon Design Associates 26, 58, 67, 155,
   157
Dimensional Stone Signs 117

Don Bell and Company 78
Douglas Williams Woodcarving 6, 35, 54
Dutchboy Signs 135

EEC Industries, Ltd. 98
Enseicom Signs, Inc. 119
Envirographics, Inc. 83, 84
Exeter Signworks 102
Expressions Advertising 75

Fantasy-in-Iron (all except Bullwhackers
   and Diamond Lil's) 94
Federal Sign 12, 22, 42
Festival Sign Service 139
Fox-Suarez Signs 52
Freeby Studios 69
Fullmoon Signs and Graphics 27

GAR Industries, Inc. (metalwork) 100
Gable Signs and Graphics, Inc. 84
Garrity Carved Signs Co. 40
Gemini Sign and Design Ltd. 64
General Sign 132
GlassArt Design 94
Glensign 23
Gordon Sign Company 80
Graphitek of Vermont, Inc. 55
Grate Signs, Inc. 28

Hannaman Sign Crafters 48, 63, 71
Hearlwood Signs 136
Heath Sign Co. 11, 56
Hoboken Sign Shop 113, 118, 125, 137
Hulme-Ridgeway Neon Sign Company 105

Imperial Sign Company 6, 60
Independent Sign Co. 40, 123
Ins-Tent Manufacturing Company 85
Interstate Neon Co. 97
Ireland and Peachey 88
Ireland, Peachey and Company 68, 73

Jansen, Robert 141
Jay Cooke's Sign Shop 26
Jim Ingram Signs 105
Jim Rizzo 109
John Chrisman 138
John Peachey and Associates 65, 116

Kate Clifford Signs 153

Lackner Sign 16
Lawry Sign, Inc. 31
Lohre and Associates, Inc. 155
Luttmann Brothers Woodcarving and
   Sign Co. 18, 22, 79, 80, 85
Luttmann, John 66

MW Reklameprodukties 152
Maineline Graphics 62
Mark Oatis Designs 110
McHale's Sign Service 72
Mercury Neon 72
Meyer Sign Co., Inc. 20
Meyer, Patrick D. 141
Miller Signs 47, 59
Morgan Sign Co. 91, 149

Natural Graphics, Inc. 11, 85, 90
Neon Fabrications 46
Neon Products, Ltd. 53
New England Sign Carvers 65

Oatis, Mark 97, 122
Oklahoma Sign Co., Inc. 93
On Board Signs 45
Openwood Studios, Inc. 68
Orange Outdoor Advertising, Inc. 145
Orde Advertising Co. 29
Orlando Forge, Inc. 98
Otter Creek Industries, Inc. 55
Outdoor Dimensions 7, 13, 20, 72

Pacific Neon Co. 130
Paul McCarthy's Carving Place 15, 126,
   130
Phoenix Zoo Design Department, The 100,
   156
Planet Neon Signs and Lighting 62, 78
Progressive Image 21

Queen City Awning 44

Rainbow-Down, The 49, 76
Rapid Sign 13
Rapid Sign of Florida, Inc. 120
Reed Design Associates 109
RTKL Associates, Inc. 97, 122
Rustic Designs 25, 115

S&S Sign Company 103
Saxton Sign Co. 36
Schmidt Metal Fabricators 100
Scott's Signs 8
Sellers, Cecil 97
Shakespeare Signs 82, 88
Sharper Images 44, 143

Sicon Group/Adtronics, The 32
Sign Crafters, Inc. 8
Sign Design Studios 129
Sign Service Co. 19, 70
Sign and Design 99
SignArt 94
Signage, Inc. 30, 65
Signcrafters 49
Signdrafters Outdoor Display, Inc. 60
Signs by Liza 134
Signs of Distinction 114, 142
Signtech Electrical Advertising, Inc. 115,
   121, 126
Signtific Signs 79
Signworks, The 76, 132, 140, 147, 148,
   152
Signworks Design and Production, Inc. 74
Signworld 35, 38, 46
Signwright 15, 30, 53
Smith, Nelson and Oatis 12, 40, 56, 94,
   97, 106, 108, 117, 122, 123, 136,
   145-147, 149, 150
SmithCraft Manufacturing Co., Inc. 68, 92
Snyder, Phil 150
Son Signs 144
Spanjer Brothers, Inc. 41
Spaz Graphix 129
Stonegraphics 75
Strictly Neon 113
Studio, The 100
Surfside Signs 34, 47, 95
Swatzenduber Signs 133

Taylor, Kas 116
Thorough-Graphic Signs 107, 123, 129
Trade-Marx Sign and Display 93, 95
Triangle Sign and Service 50
TubeArt 34, 87

Ultra Neon 118
Ultraneon Sign Co. 104, 110
Uxbridge Carvers 51

Vince Rogers Signs 21
Vintage Sign Shoppe 124
Vital Signs 37, 67, 112, 157

Walt Disney Imageering 107
Walt Disney World Mill Shop 128
Watermark 140
Weaver, Keith 150
Wood Shop, The 86
Wood Signs 153
Wood and Wood Sign Co. 36, 37, 43, 52,
   61, 69, 96, 99, 122, 154
Woodmark 23, 80

Yancey Sign Art, Inc. 25
Yaseen Design Studio 39

ALSO AVAILABLE FROM ROCKPORT PUBLISHERS

Rockport Publishers, Inc., 146 Granite Street, Rockport, Massachusetts 01966, TEL: (508) 546-9590, FAX: (508) 546-7141

TYPE & COLOR: A Handbook of Creative Combinations

Graphic artists must perform quickly, creatively and accurately. Type & Color enables graphic artists to spec type in color quickly and efficiently. Eleven sheets of color type styles printed on acetate overlays can be combined with hundreds of color bars, making it possible to experiment with thousands of color/type combinations right at the drawing board. In minutes, your eye will rapidly judge what the mind had conceived. 160 pages plus 11 pages of acetate overlays.

160 Pages + 11 acetates   Hardcover

$34.95   ISBN 0-935603-19-0

TYPE & COLOR 2: Fades

In the process of creating new graphic design ideas, one constantly confronts the problem of results that do not match the original concept. Often this happens when the designer does not have sufficient control of the reproduction process and must make decisions based on limited understanding of the possibilities. A perfect example of this is the use of graduated color fades as background behind graphics, objects, or text.

To answer this concern, we have developed TYPE & COLOR 2. This book is a tool that not only shows the effects of various color gradations but also provides the breakdown of process colors that were used to achieve the effect. As an added graphic aid, we have included two acetates printed with various lines of type in ten different opaque colors to show how color type works within a graduated color background.

128 Pages   Hardcover

$24.95   ISBN 1-56496-065-X

TYPE IN PLACE: A Thumbnail Approach to Creative Type Placement

This companion guide to Type & Color includes 11 acetates with printed type for use with thumbnail images in the book. With this tool, designers can easily envision in thumbnail, ideas for type placement with sample layouts included in the text. This new system allows designers to start from scratch in designing type placements rather than to start from the point of imitation. 60 pages of examples of great type placements are also included.

160 Pages + 11 acetates   Hardcover

$34.95   ISBN 0-935603-87-5

CD PACKAGING & GRAPHICS 2: The Best Promotional and Retail Packaging

A follow up to the highly-successful first edition, this new book presents the most inspiring designs for the latest in music packaging and media. The CD format has come into its own, and CD packaging has evolved into a flourishing art form. Included are CD covers, CD booklets, screen-printed images on CDs, and unusual and innovative packaging designs. This book features the best work by prominent U.S. and international designers. It is an excellent sourcebook of graphic design, package design, typography, illustration, photography, and printing techniques. Collectors, music aficionados, even vinyl loyalists will find new and innovative takes on music packaging.

192 Pages   Hardcover

$39.95   ISBN 1-56496-068-4

THE CREATIVE STROKE: Communication with Brush and Pen in Graphic Design

This book presents an in-depth look at the most creative and innovative uses of freehand imagery in design, specifically those with brush and pen. While the current push for computer-generated graphics has revolutionized the design industry, there is a renewed interest in the uniqueness of the freehand, especially since once produced, the images can be scanned into the computer. Designers can use thos book to refer to what's currently being produced in both brush/pen graphics and calligraphy. Materials includes Media Advertising, Direct Mail, Posters, Book Covers, Packaging, and Corporate ID. Experience the magic of freehand art!

192 Pages   Hardcover

$39.95   ISBN 0-935603-61-1

GRAPHIC IDEA NOTEBOOK

The new revised softcover edition of this workhorse book contains 24 all-new pages. This book is a study in graphic design, covering innovative problem- solving, demonstrating techniques to turn routine material into provocative editorial presentation.

216 Pages   Softcover

$18.95   ISBN 0-935603-64-6

MIX & MATCH DESIGNER'S COLORS

Produced by a designer for designers, this book incorporates several features aimed at minimizing guesswork and eliminating errors that are often experienced when using traditional methods of choosing tints for use in four- color process. Extra large swatches show the color extremely clearly, and the ability to turn them over individually allows colors to be compared. From each swatch, the designer can see a variety of color percentages, both knock out and overprint type will appear on that tint, and also how a halftone image appears printed in that color.

300 Swatches   Hardcover

$34.95   ISBN 1-56496-009-9

COLOR HARMONY 2: 1,000 New Color Combinations for the Designer

The new companion book to COLOR HARMONY (which is already in its ninth printing) is the latest step-by-step guide to choosing and combining colors for graphic designers, artists, hobbyists, fashion designers, interior decorators, and anyone else who works with color. COLOR HARMONY 2 contains new and exciting color combinations, all laid out in easy-to-read swatches and accompanied by color photographs of these new color schemes in action. Select just the right combination to convey a mood or create a dynamic impression from the largest and most thorough color guide available.

160 Pages   Softcover

$15.95   ISBN 1-56496-066-8

3-DIMENSIONAL ILLUSTRATORS AWARDS ANNUAL IV

The latest series of full-color 3-dimensional illustrations from the Fourth Annual Dimensional Illustrators Awards Show. This year's awards show was better and larger than ever, with an international attendance and categories that included Paper Sculpture, Paper Collage, Clay Sculpture, Fabric Collage, Wood Sculpture, Plastic Sculpture, Mixed Media, and Singular Mediums. 3-D IV is a state-of-the-art sourcebook that offers the most extensive collection of its kind in one magnificent volume.

256 Pages   Hardcover

$59.95   ISBN 1-56496-058-7

AIRBRUSH ACTION 2: The Best New Airbrush Illustration

This remarkable collection, compiled by Airbrush Action Magazine and Rockport Publishers, boasts the most unique group of airbrush work by the top US airbrush illustrators ever assembled. Introducing the definitive volume of airbrush images that range from the sublime to the humorous. This full-color book exhibits over 400 carefully selected works.

AIRBRUSH ACTION 2 also features an insightful introduction by Clifford Stieglitz, publisher of Airbrush Action magazine.

192 Pages   Hardcover

$34.95   ISBN 1-56496-067-6

LABEL DESIGN 4: The Best New U.S. and International Design

LABEL DESIGN 3 was critically acclaimed for its unique editorial and reproduction quality. LABEL DESIGN 4 continues that excellence. It is a showcase of the best up-to-the-minute work in label designs. Labels from the following areas will be included: food, snacks, beverages, wines, beer, liquor, health and beauty aids, consumer goods, media products, and much more. Award-winning package designs from all over the world are featured in this full-color sourcebook. This homage to contemporary labels provides useful inspiration to the packaging designer.

240 Pages   Hardcover

$49.95   ISBN 1-56496-069-2

GRAPHIC DESIGN: CHICAGO

Following the successful format of GRAPHIC DESIGN: NEW YORK, this new full-color volume pays an overdue homage to the top design talent working in the Windy City today. This midwestern metropolis graces us with some of the most formidable creativity today, including the work of Thirst, Concrete Design, Liska Associates, and Lipson Associates. The carefully selected firms have been chosen based upon their distinctive contributions to consumer, corporate, and publication design. The talent showcased here transcends "regional" boundaries and explores new frontiers in design.

224 Pages   Hardcover

$49.95   ISBN 1-56496-071-4

THE BEST OF COLORED PENCIL 2

This richly illustrated book showcases the best submissions from the first Colored Pencil Society of America Competition. Also included are selections from members of the Society that display a broad range of subjects and styles. From photo-realistic renderings to abstracts and graphic illustrations, this book captures the medium's versatility for creating "drawings" and "paintings."

This definitive collection demonstrates why the humble pencil has gone beyond preliminary sketches and outlines and taken its place in the world of professional illustration and fine art. More than an introduction to colored pencils, this book features the ultimate results obtainable with a dry pigment.

THE BEST OF COLORED PENCIL 2 is a comprehensive reference for the professional or emerging artist/illustrator and is an important sourcebook for designers and art directors.

160 Pages   Hardcover

$24.95   ISBN 1-56496-072-2

LETTERHEAD & LOGO DESIGNS 2 Creating the Corporate Image

The most exciting and effective current designs for corporate identity packages including letterheads, business cards, envelopes, and stationery supplies are presented. LETTERHEAD & LOGO DESIGNS 2 showcases the latest in ideas for the graphic designer looking to create a corporate image. This definitive full-color volume offers effective concepts that create dazzling corporate campaigns.

256 pages   Hardcover

$49.95   ISBN 1-56496-006-4

DESKTOP PUBLISHER'S EASY TYPE GUIDE: The 150 Most Important Typefaces

There are thousands of different type styles available to the owners of desktop publishing systems, and more being created daily. How does one choose which to purchase? This book will not only help you make those decisions, but will show you how to get the most benefit from the type styles you choose. From the neophyte designer, to the desktop newcomer this guide will prove a valuable resource.

176 Pages   Softcover

$19.95   ISBN 1-56496-007-2

COMPUTER GRAPHICS: The Best Computer Art & Design

The talent in this volume will astonish and inspire every designer. This tribute to electronic design reveals how computers have revolutionized the look of today's media. Categories include Magazines, Packaging, Posters, Broadcast Design, Fine Arts, Technical Illustration, and much more. Several techniques are presented and explored, such as scanned and manipulated photographs, drawings, illustrations, and graphic designs. This book features work from over 100 of the most talented designers, illustrators, and fine artists working with state-of-the-art electronic design systems.

160 Pages   Softcover

$34.95   I   SBN 1-56496-015-3